The
Christian Doctrine
of the
Divine Attributes

The
Christian Doctrine
of the
Divine Attributes

Hermann Cremer

Foreword by
Matthias Gockel

Edited by
Helmut Burkhardt

Translated by
Robert B. Price

☙PICKWICK *Publications* · Eugene, Oregon

THE CHRISTIAN DOCTRINE OF THE DIVINE ATTRIBUTES

Pickwick Publications
An Imprint of Wipf and Stock Publishers
199 W. 8th Ave., Suite 3
Eugene, OR 97401

www.wipfandstock.com

PAPERBACK ISBN 13: 978-1-4982-0123-0
HARDCOVER ISBN 13: 978-1-4982-8543-8
EBOOK ISBN: 978-1-4982-0124-7

Cataloguing-in-Publication data:

Names: Cremer, Hermann, 1834–1903.

Title: The Christian doctrine of the divine attributes / Hermann Cremer; translated by Robert B. Price.

Description: Eugene, OR: Pickwick Publications, 2016 | Includes indexes.

Identifiers: ISBN 978-1-4982-0123-0 (paperback) | ISBN 978-1-4982-8543-8 (hardcover) | ISBN 978-1-4982-0124-7 (ebook)

Subjects: LCSH: God (Christianity)—Attributes | Revelation—Christianity | Theology, Doctrinal | Price, Robert B. | Gockel, Matthias. | Title

Classification: LCC: BT130 C746 2016 (paperback) | BT130 (ebook)

Manufactured in the U.S.A.   05/17/16

Contents

Foreword

For more than a century, Hermann Cremer's treatise on the Christian doctrine of God's attributes lay dormant and its wealth went undetected. Its originality was noted and praised by important Protestant voices in the 20th century, but only in recent years have theologians in Europe and North America begun to probe its contents in detail.[1] The present translation and publication should be applauded as a sign of renewed interest in innovative doctrinal theology. The topic is highly relevant not only for Christian self-reflection but also for contemporary interreligious debates with Judaism and Islam.

Cremer integrates a wide range of biblical writings into his thinking, without using them simply as proof-texts. His widespread image as a "positive" theologian should be treated with caution. He did not adhere to a quasi-objective view of Holy Scripture or religious experience. One should rather regard him as an early representative of Biblical Theology (a label, to be sure, that can be understood in many ways).

Cremer's treatise boldly declares that there is "no excuse" to continue in the "old ruts" (page 5 below). Indeed, he anticipates a number of theological developments in the 20th century. His focus lies on God's revelatory acting out of love (*Liebeshandeln*) to save human beings from sin and death. God's self-revelation is the one common source of all divine attributes. Cremer thus rejects the traditional distinctions between 'ontological' and 'economic' or transcendent and immanent attributes. His own distinction between two series of attributes is meant logically, not ontologically. The first series includes the attributes related to God the Redeemer

---

1. For further discussion of the treatise and its reception, see Matthias Gockel, "Hermann Cremers Umformung der christlichen Lehre von den Eigenschaften Gottes im Lichte ihrer Rezeption im 20. Jahrhundert," *Neue Zeitschrift für Systematische Theologie und Religionsphilosophie* 56 (2014) 35–63.

in Jesus Christ (holiness, righteousness, and wisdom), the second series the attributes related to God the Creator in light of his self-disclosure in Jesus Christ (omnipotence, omnipresence or world-presence, omniscience, eternity and immutability).[2] Cremer's choice of attributes is mirrored in Karl Barth's doctrine of divine "perfections" in *Church Dogmatics* II/1. Barth adds complexity and breadth to the doctrine, but he clearly remains indebted to Cremer in many ways.[3]

Moreover, the treatise pays particular attention to the attribute of righteousness. Cremer criticizes the 17th century Protestant understanding of this attribute in terms of the Greek concept of justice as Highest Virtue. He rejects the widespread view of divine righteousness as penal justice (*Strafgerechtigkeit*), as if there were an opposition between righteousness and mercy. In contrast, he emphasizes that God's grace liberates the sinner not apart from but in and through God's judgment: forgiveness is "not a salvation *from* his hand, but a salvation *through* his hand" (31).

In sum, although one may criticize some aspects of Cremer's argument,[4] his treatise raises questions that still stand at the heart of Christian theology in the early twenty-first century. We can be grateful to Rob Price for his labor of love and the excellent translation of Cremer's text. Let us hope that it receives the careful attention it deserves.

Matthias Gockel
Friedrich-Schiller-University Jena

---

2. Helmut Burkhardt thinks that Cremer's redemption-centered approach leaves no room for the recognition of God's beneficent activity as creator (xix). His criticism overlooks the fact that for Cremer creation comprehends nature as well as history. The main problem lies elsewhere: Cremer's *Dogmatische Prinzipienlehre* assumes a second source of human knowledge of God besides God's self-revelation and thus a "natural theology of conscience." Cf. Gockel, "Cremers Umformung," 39–40, 61–63.

3. See the meticulous analysis by Robert B. Price, *Letters of the Divine Word: The Perfections of God in Karl Barth's Church Dogmatics* (London: T. & T. Clark, 2011).

4. Cf. Gockel, "Cremers Umformung," 58–63.

Introduction

THE ATTRIBUTES OF GOD

We live in a time that has forgotten who God is. So we are no longer certain of the fact that he exists. As a result, we live as if there were no God.

Some say that this forgetfulness of God got stuck in our heads from the influence of the philosophy of Kant, who claimed that God is not a possible object of knowledge, but only its postulate.[1]

But would it actually be desirable to have God as the mere object of human knowing? Would it be responsible to put God, the creator and Lord of the world, under the microscope of our theological science? To extract "attributes" from him with the dissecting knife of our logic, and classify them according to the models of our conceptuality? Would this not be a kind of *crimen laesae majestatis*, an affront to the majesty of God?

On the other hand, what would it actually mean for faith if believers did not know the one whom they believe? What if the grounds and, be it said, object of faith withdrew to the darkness of an abstraction concerning the sheer facticity of the existence of God?

Melanchthon once opined that the question of all questions is whether or not God exists.[2] While this is indeed true in certain respects, it is only half so. For even an affirmative answer to this question would be empty in itself. It would say more or less nothing, as long as we could not also say

---

1. K. H. Michel, *Immanuel Kant und die Frage der Erkennbarkeit Gottes* (Wuppertal: Brockhaus, 1987).

2. H. Engelland, *Die Wirklichkeit Gottes und die Gewißheit des Glaubens* (Göttingen: Vandenhoeck und Ruprecht, 1966) 7.

precisely who it is upon whom I am supposed to base my entire life, with all my aspirations and efforts.

The question concerning "the attributes of God" is a question concerning what identifies God as God, as the God of Israel and Father of Jesus Christ, and so enables us to know him. It is no mere textbook treatment of some traditional theme of theology, but a central question of Christian faith and therefore of theology as an academic discipline.

These connections have not always been made clear in the past, and in general neither have they been today. The apparently purely speculative question concerning the attributes of God is generally thrust to the margins of theology, or reduced to or reinterpreted as a question concerning the subjective determination of our "feeling of absolute dependence."[3]

Cremer sought to lift this doctrine out of its poor Cinderella existence by dedicating to it what has to this day remained one of its most thorough expositions. Though it has often been cited in the theological literature since its publication, few have known of it by more than hearsay. Even the author himself is generally known only as the author of the forerunner to the *Theological Dictionary of the New Testament*, the "Cremer-Kögel," the *Biblico-Theological Lexicon of New Testament Greek*. Cremer is categorized as an exegete, not as the theologian—though theologian he was and showed himself to be in his examination of the doctrine of the divine attributes.

CREMER'S LIFE

August Hermann Cremer was born October 18, 1834, in Unna in Westphalia. He died October 4, 1903 in Greifswald in Pomerania. He belonged to an old Westphalian family of farmers. His father was a teacher and had been influenced by the spiritual life of the awakening in Germany at the beginning of the nineteenth century. There was little formal organization in these groups of awakened believers, but a broad network of personal relationships. The parents of Friedrich von Bodelschwingh, among others, were also among the awakened Christians who met in Unna.

Cremer's mother, née Josephson, came from a Jewish family for whom the Jewish emancipation at the end of the eighteenth century had meant both assimilation to Christian culture as well as "the entryway to living

---

3. Schleiermacher, *The Christian Faith*, §50, thesis; cf. Cremer, *Divine Attributes*, 1.

faith."[4] From childhood Cremer grew up amidst a lively piety that was nourished by the Bible.

His first high school, in Dortmund, was poorly led and much disturbed by the revolutionary spirit of the day, and his time there was hardly satisfying. Much more fruitful was his attendance at the newly founded Christian high school in Gütersloh. While in Gütersloh (1851–53), during a visit with relatives in Solingen, Cremer also became acquainted with a group of awakened Christians. It had been established by the medical doctor Samuel Collenbusch (1724–1803), one of the influential figures of pietism as it transitioned into the awakening. Collenbusch's ideas gave Cremer for the first time the deep "impression that knowledge of the content of Scripture has in many, not insignificant ways left behind what the work of the church has drawn from Scripture, so that here there is still much land to occupy."[5] Although Cremer's engagement with Collenbusch's thought was certainly not uncritical, he continued it for the rest of his life. Even the year before he died, Cremer edited a collection of Collenbusch's writings[6] and documented in the introduction Collenbusch's significant influence on the theology of the nineteenth century, particularly on the so-called Erlangen School.

After graduating, Cremer continued his studies in Halle (1853–56) under August Tholuck (1799–1877), then in Tübingen (1856–57) under Johann Tobias Beck (1804–78). Under the influence of Beck, biblicism ultimately became "the dominant feature of his theology," and from Tholuck he learned "to classify the contents of Scripture according to the contrast between sin and grace."[7] After Cremer passed his first exam, the publisher Steinkopf financed his promotion to the licentiate of theology in Tübingen on the basis of his study on Jesus' Olivet Discourse in Matthew 24–25.[8] At the same time, following a suggestion by Tholuck, Cremer began the research for his *Biblico-Theological Lexicon*. In his year in Tübingen he also struck up the friendship with Martin Kähler (1835–1912) that would last the rest of their lives.

---

4. Ernst Cremer, *Hermann Cremer: Ein Lebens- und Charakterbild* (Gütersloh: Bertelsmann, 1912) 3.

5. E. Cremer, *Hermann Cremer*, 15–16.

6. Hermann Cremer, ed., *Aus dem Nachlaß eines Gottesgelehrten: Aufsätze, Briefe und Tagebuchblätter von Dr. Samuel Collenbusch* (Stuttgart: Steinkopf, 1902).

7. E. Cremer, *Hermann Cremer*, 20.

8. H. Cremer, *Die eschatologische Rede Jesu Christi Matthäi 24–25: Versuch einer exegetischen Erörterung derselben* (Stuttgart: Steinkopf, 1860).

While Kähler, upon completion of his studies, and with his parents' financial support, immediately set out on an academic career and became Tholuck's assistant, Cremer's path led him first to the pastorate. Although gifting and inclination drew him strongly to academic work, he threw himself into his work as preacher and pastor in the rural community of Ostönnen in Soest, while continuing to work on his *Lexicon* with ceaseless devotion. The intensive research, particularly on the concepts *dikaios, dikaioun,* and *dikaiosune* led him away from Beck's (and also Collenbusch's) understanding of justification and back to a biblically and exegetically grounded, reformational understanding, which had also proven itself in his experience as preacher of the gospel. The righteousness of God is his saving, judging intervention for all who trust in him.[9] The *Lexicon* was completed in 1866 and was a major publishing success. It went through nine editions in Cremer's lifetime, every one of them painstakingly revised and expanded by Cremer himself.

It was at this point that the theological world finally became aware of Cremer. This led eventually—and over the vehement objections of the liberal Protestantenverein—to his appointment in 1870 to the theological faculty of the University of Greifswald as professor of systematic theology.

Cremer remained in this position for the rest of his life. Cremer's professorship was bound with the pastorate of a church in Greifswald, where he served until 1890. Cremer was offered prestigious chairs at the Universities of Leipzig (1892 and 1894) and Berlin (1892 and 1897). These he declined, feeling that God had personally tasked him with developing a unified "positive" faculty in the small university town of Greifswald—"a place where the gospel might survive the winter," as he liked to say.[10]

Cremer understood his work at Greifswald as involving a twofold aim. First, his entire life's work marched under the banner of defensive action against the rational or later so-called liberal theology of the school of Albrecht Ritschl (1822–89). In a 1901 letter to Schlatter he wrote:

> Infinitely much is at stake. The inclination toward Berlin that rules the senior church hierarchy and at court, that can be summarized in the phrase, "No controversy, please!" and that expects us to join

9. See Cremer's great work, *Die paulinische Rechtfertigungslehre im Zusammenhang ihrer geschichtlichen Voraussetzungen* (Gütersloh: Bertelsmann, 1899, 1900²).

10. E.g., in a letter to Martin Kähler, July 18, 1894, in E. Cremer, *Hermann Cremer,* 153; likewise to Adolf Schlatter, December 30, 1897, in Robert Stupperich, ed., *Hermann Cremer—Haupt der "Greifswalder Schule": Briefwechsel und Dokumente* (Cologne: Böhlau, 1988) 417.

together with all these people—it will surely come to ruin. May God help us to emphasize again and again, so loudly that everyone hears: the decision depends on the question, or rather, on the fact of sin. Sin is either opposition to the will of God which fundamentally destroys us, or it is just a mistake, so that our consciousness of guilt because of sin is likewise just a mistake. It is a matter of winning the verdict on revelation. God requires that we believe in revelation, either in the most unbelievable gift he gives us or in the undreamt of but not unbelievable unveiling of what is still called grace. Every word and concept they empty of its particular, original content, but they continue to use it. Thus the same drama takes place before our eyes that we encountered in the ancient church. The same words, but the opposite meaning! And yet it is disastrous to go about coining new words.

Oh how deeply the basic character of this movement touches me! It does away with every achievement of the Reformation, *everything*, yet still calls itself reformational and Protestant. Do we not still have a living God, who, as freely as we and more freely still, lives out a history with us and for us? Do we not have a Savior, come from heaven and brought down to us, who in his humiliation belongs to us and by his resurrection remains eternally our own? Is not our sole hope of salvation belief in the unbelievable but real? Is there not a continuation of personal, individual life after death? Everything, absolutely everything is being taken from us. In exchange, we are offered a variety of "scholarly achievements," until we arrive back at the point from which our fathers set out—the bosom of the Catholic Church and the individual's absolute insecurity and uncertainty. Therefore: Let the witness be bold. Again: Let the witness be bold![11]

Cremer's second aim was his positive struggle to reconstruct a theology that was more deeply rooted in the Bible itself. Together with Kähler and later with Schlatter he represented "the ideal of a theology renewed by closer connection to Scripture and richer exposition of its doctrinal content."[12] In a letter to Steinkopf in 1895 he wrote:

Our faculty is now entirely unified in composition, as hardly ever a faculty in Germany this century has been, other than Erlangen. But we differ from Erlangen in this: for Erlangen it is the confession that is paramount; for us it is the Bible. If one must put a

11. Letter to Adolf Schlatter, January 30, 1901, in Stupperich, ed., *Hermann Cremer,* 432–33.

12. E. Cremer, *Hermann Cremer,* 142.

label on it, what we represent is the Bengelian Style, the Bengelian School. God help us![13]

One particular highlight of Cremer's endeavors, indeed, of his entire life, as he himself acknowledged, was his close working relationship with Adolf Schlatter (1852–1938), who was called to a New Testament professorship in Greifswald in 1888. Despite the differing confessional allegiance and the intellectual independence of both men, they came together as fruitful co-laborers in a selfless effort to bring about a biblically renewed theology. Though Schlatter followed a call in 1893 to a newly established chair in systematic theology in Berlin, their partnership did not end. Their crowning achievement came in 1897 with the founding of the journal *Beiträge zur Förderung christlicher Theologie (Contributions to the Promotion of Christian Theology)*.[14] Over the coming decades many worthwhile— and still worthwhile—contributions would appear here, seeking theological reconstruction that would combine academic breadth with congregational relevance, contemporary awareness with biblical perspective.

Cremer's own first contribution came in the first year of the journal, presented here as *The Christian Doctrine of the Divine Attributes*. In 1900 appeared his "Prophecy and Miracle in the History of Salvation." In 1903, shortly before his death, Cremer expressed deep concern about the direction theology was taking in "The Basic Truths of Christianity According to Reinhold Seeberg." In this piece he warned of the seduction of the so-called "modern-positive" theology, which was slipping almost imperceptibly from confessional Lutheranism toward Ritschl.[15] Posthumously there appeared Cremer's "Pastoral Theology" (1904)[16] and "On Work and Property" (1907).[17]

13. Letter to Friedrich Steinkopf, March 8, 1895, in Stupperich, ed., *Hermann Cremer*, 87 (cf. E. Cremer, *Hermann Cremer*, 155).

14. Cf. E. Cremer, *Hermann Cremer*, 268; Adolf Schlatter, "Die Entstehung der *Beiträge zur Förderung christlicher Theologie*," *Beiträge zur Förderung christlicher Theologie* 25, no. 1 (1920) esp. 71ff.

15. See also Cremer's letter to Schlatter, February 15, 1898, on the occation of Seeberg's appointment as Schlatter's successor in Berlin, in Stupperich, ed., *Hermann Cremer*, 67–68.

16. J. Ohlemacher, "Was sind geistliche 'Voraussetzungen' für ein 'geistliches Amt'? Nachdenkliches aus Anlass des 100. Todestages von Hermann Cremer," *Theologische Beiträge* 35 (2004) 140–52.

17. Cremer, "Über Arbeit und Eigentum nach christlicher Anschauung: Eine Vorlesung," *Beiträge zur Förderung christlicher Theologie* 11, no. 3 (1907) 35–56; repr., Hermann Cremer, *Arbeit und Eigentum in christlicher Sicht*, ed. H. Burkhardt (Gießen: Brunnen, 1984) 7–23.

The latter study comes from yet another area of Cremer's work, one still less known today, his engagement with the social question. In this essay he extended a claim already made in an 1889 essay, "The Influence of the Christian Principle of Love on Legal Development and Legislation,"[18] namely, that the dominant Roman-law concept of property that underlies capitalism contradicts the Christian principle of love. It leaves property to the caprice of the owner and allows at best private expressions of love. But the poor must not only be granted a right to charity. Social legislation must procure property for them, so that they are no longer dependent on charity.[19]

His engagement with the social question brought Cremer into close contact with Adolf Stöcker (1835–1909), the Berlin city missionary and social politician. In 1894, at a Frankfurt conference of the Evangelical Social Congress, which Stöcker had co-founded, Cremer presented a paper alongside his theological opponent Adolf von Harnack (1851–1930). On "The Social Question and Preaching" Cremer explained:

> A Protestant minister is the last one who may be permitted to stand idly before the social question and just wait to see how things turn out. Even if this question had only an economic-political dimension, and only had to do with the distribution of material interests, the preacher of the gospel, the servant of the church of Jesus Christ, is the born champion of the poor and oppressed. He must look after those who sigh under the weight of need and misery. He ought to be the first to exert himself for the improvement of their condition.[20]

No less insistently, however, did Cremer warn against overblown aspirations and expectations. "Awareness of the worldly utility of Christianity repeatedly suggests that an imposing church, a Christian majority, will be a means of attracting people. And then, surely, we will find truly converted Christians." "No," said Cremer. "We must preach as if we actually wanted to convert the entire world, and as if we had to want this. But we must be perfectly clear in our own minds that, the more clearly we preach, the more

---

18. Reprint in Cremer, *Arbeit und Eigentum*, ed. Burkhardt, 23–34. In a letter to A. Stöcker (in Stupperich, ed., *Hermann Cremer*, 335), Cremer wrote that this brief publication had "earned him the reputation of a Social Democrat in disguise."

19. E. Cremer, *Hermann Cremer*, 185–86.

20. In *Bericht über die Verhandlungen des Fünften Evangelisch-sozialen Kongresses, abgehalten zu Frankfurt am Main am 16. und 17. Mai 1894. Nach den stenographischen Protokollen* (Berlin: Rehtwisch und Langewort, 1894) 11–22; repr., Cremer, *Arbeit und Eigentum*, ed. Burkhardt, 34–47, esp. 36; cf. E. Cremer, *Hermann Cremer*, 203.

clearly will decision be called for. And the decision of cultural Christians will mostly be a decision *against* the gospel."[21]

It was not only writings, however, that were the fruit of Cremer's decades of courageous and tireless work in Greifswald. Above all it was people. First of all there were the students, who came to Greifswald in rapidly growing numbers, not only from Pomerania but soon from across Germany. Cremer became their leader and guided them to an enduring understanding of theology. Not infrequently he counseled them personally as well. There were also, and not least, the young theologians, who took inspiration from Cremer for their own academic work. Soon people everywhere were speaking of a "Greifswald School." But it was not a school in the sense of possessing a common system of thought, recognizable in constantly repeated slogans. Its commonality consisted rather in a common endeavor to produce a theology born out of a fresh hearing of the whole of Scripture.

The most well-known of Cremer's students were Erich Schaeder (1861–1936; major work, *Theocentric Theology*, 2 vols., 1909–14) and especially Wilhelm Lütgert (1867–1938), of independent and enduring significance as an exegete (e.g., *The Proclamation of Freedom and the Fanatical Spirits in Corinth*, 1908), as a historian (*The Religion of German Idealism and its End*, 4 vols., 1922–30), and as a theologian (*Creation and Revelation*, 1934; reprint Gießen, 1984, with an introduction by Werner Neuer; and *The Ethics of Love*, 1938). Julius Kögel (1871–1928) extended Cremer's work on the *Lexicon*. Even Kähler's student Julius Schniewind took enduring inspiration from Cremer.[22]

CREMER'S CONTRIBUTION[23]

What then is Cremer's particular contribution to the Christian doctrine of the divine attributes? Cremer begins his enquiry with the observation that

---

21. Letter to Martin Kähler, January 5, 1899, in E. Cremer, *Hermann Cremer*, 219–20. See the letters to Stöcker himself in Stupperich, ed., *Hermann Cremer*, 335–39; cf. E. Cremer, *Hermann Cremer*, 197–200, where E. Cremer mistakenly places the letter from May 17, 1895 after that of June 12.

22. Gerhard Friedrich, "Julius Schniewind, ein Lehrer der Kirche," in *Evangelische Theologie* 43 (1983) 202–21, esp. 215–18 on Cremer.

23. See Martin Pfizenmaier, "Der Beitrag Hermann Cremers zur Lehre von den Eigenschaften Gottes," in *Wer ist das—Gott?*, ed. Helmut Burkhardt (Gießen: Brunnen, 1982) 133–41.

the doctrine of the divine attributes is in an enduring crisis. His contribution extends both to the diagnosis as well as to the treatment of this crisis.

The crisis is especially clear in the gaping divergence between the faith of the local congregation, for whom knowledge of the being and attributes of God is indispensable (xxi), and academic theology, which finds itself increasingly unable to adhere to this doctrine. This inability of academic theology has religious grounds that, on the basis of its presuppositions, are to be taken entirely seriously (2). However—and this is Cremer's decisive criticism—it is precisely these presuppositions that are wrong. Academic theology assumes that the concept of God in Greek philosophy, that of Pure Being or The Absolute, is applicable to the God of the Bible (3-4). According to Cremer, this appropriation of the Greek concept of God comes from asking the wrong basic question. Greek philosophy concerns itself with the riddle of the world posed to us by nature, by conditioned being. The actual riddle, however, is the riddle of history that bursts forth from the judgment of conscience (4): How can there exist a world if, according to the law of sin and death that reigns within it, it must perish?

According to Cremer, the answer to this question can only be found in God's revelation of himself attested in the Bible (4-5). In the Bible, God shows himself "as the one who is entirely love" (8). But from this understanding of the being of God, the divine attributes cannot just be deduced by logical necessity (according to "the law of consistency" which Cremer constantly attacks). For love is an essentially free act and is therefore opposed to every necessity. To describe individual attributes of God, we thus depend on historical testimony to revelation. What we find here is that the attributes of God are "the determination of his action by his essence" (8).

In this way Cremer affirms the sovereignty of the living God of the Bible, while still making definite assertions about the attributes of God, and not merely about the attributes of religious feeling (Schleiermacher). Cremer manages on the whole to stick to the reality of God without reducing him to an idea, both in faith and in theology. Cremer thus identifies the attributes of which the Christian doctrine of God speaks as the attributes of God revealed in Christ. Accordingly, Cremer's account begins with a series of divine attributes disclosed in revelation: holiness, righteousness, and wisdom. He then examines a second series of attributes, those that are "implicit in the concept of God" itself (and also acknowledged in other religions): omnipotence, omnipresence, omniscience, and immutability. These latter, however, are only considered "in light of revelation." That is, their content is derived not from the concept of God but from the biblical revelation that incorporates the concept of God, thus filling them with fresh content.

By tying himself to the Bible, Cremer overcomes scholasticism's dependence on the Greek concept of God, without lapsing into liberal theology's dissolution of the idea of God.

Despite many positive references to Cremer in modern theology,[24] the still long-awaited reception of Cremer's work will certainly not be able to overlook possible weaknesses. Cremer's latter decades were spent in constant struggle against the triumph of Ritschlian theology. This struggle made Cremer one of the most insightful readers of Ritschl's theology. But the ongoing debate, though sharply critical, was not entirely without repercussions on Cremer's own position. As close a friend as Schlatter points out that Cremer was more strongly under Ritschl's influence "than was, in my opinion, healthy for the strength of his theology."[25]

Among these weaknesses may belong, for instance, Cremer's concentration or limitation of the idea of revelation to the revelation of redemption. "We know God through his actual conduct, though his revelation. . .through the redemption that he offers to us" (11). Does not such a claim overlook

---

24. E.g., Karl Barth, *Church Dogmatics*, II/1:260 (an "extraordinarily informative book"), and the references, occasionally critical, on 282, 285, 299, 341, 383, 426. Emil Brunner, *Dogmatics*, trans. Olive Wyon (London: Lutterworth, 1949) 1:294: "Hermann Cremer, in particular, has rendered us a great service . . . in his outstanding small book, *Die christliche Lehre von den Eigenschaften Gottes*, as the first to have pointed out the contrast between the traditional doctrine of the divine attributes and the idea of God in the Bible . . . Twenty years ago, when I began to teach dogmatics, it was Cremer, too, who opened my eyes." Also, ibid., 297: "Cremer's trailblazing achievement." Otto Weber, *Foundations of Dogmatics*, trans. Darrell L. Guder (Grand Rapids: Eerdmans, 1981), 1:403n15 (an "important . . . monograph"); cf. ibid., 408, 455n152. Eberhard Jüngel, *God as the Mystery of the World*, trans. Darrell L. Guder (Grand Rapids: Eerdmans, 1983) 226n1, "This book merits more attention than has been given it in theological discussion." Wolfhart Pannenberg discusses Cremer's work in detail and calls it, almost one hundred years after its publication, "the most significant contribution of modern theology to the doctrine of the divine attributes" (*Systematic Theology*, trans. Geoffrey W. Bromiley (Grand Rapids: Eerdmans, 1991–1998) 1:367–68).

25. Adolf Schlatter, *Rückblick aus seine Lebensarbeit* (Gütersloh: Bertelsmann, 1952) 142. Wolfhart Pannenberg says of Cremer's work on the attributes, "The influence of the antimetaphysical character of Ritschl's doctrine of God . . . upon circles that otherwise stood apart from him was probably conveyed through Herman Cremer," in "The Appropriation of the Philosophical Concept of God as a Dogmatic Problem of Early Christian Theology," 121n9, in *Basic Questions in Theology: Collected Essays*, trans. George H. Kehm (Philadelphia: Fortress, 1971) 2:119–83.

such biblical passages as Rom 1:18–32 or Acts 14:15–16? Is not God's action as creator also "his action for us and towards us" (11)? It was in fact typical particularly of the liberal theology of the Ritschlian School (and dialectical theology of all varieties took over this heritage), under pressure from the natural sciences, to downplay nature and therefore faith in creation as well. Where the reality of creation was shuffled out of view and attention focused on history, eschatology was eventually and only too easily corrupted into a mere actualistic historicism, without continuity and hence without being.

Such a consequence was far from Cremer's own mind. But his approach concealed this danger within it. Among his students, it was especially Lütgert who recognized this and sought to overcome it.[26] That Cremer never saw creation and revelation as alternatives can be seen in his integration of the "general" attributes of God with those given in (special) revelation. It is characteristic of Cremer, for instance, that while he sees the difficulties of the concept of divine immutability, he does not simply discard it (as is common today under the banner of existentialism), but fills and coins it anew using the biblical idea of eternity (79–80).

Cremer thus leads theology to the living source of biblical knowledge. This alone would justify the republication of this work. This does not make it our task simply to adopt as formulas the insights of our theological forefathers. Rather, we must allow their insights to help and encourage us to our own insight into biblical truth in our own time. This is the great opportunity that stands before us in a man like Hermann Cremer.

READING CREMER'S TEXT

Readers without theological training will probably have some trouble understanding the first two chapters in particular. That such readers may not grow tired or give up too soon, perhaps they may be directed to begin with the third and fourth chapters, and thus with the actual presentation of the divine attributes.

Cremer's intensely concentrated study demands from the reader much dedication and patience. Only repeated reading will reveal the full riches of this work. But such perseverance will be richly rewarded.

Helmut Burkhardt
Summer 1983, revised summer 2004

---

26. Werner Neuer, foreword to the new edition of Wilhelm Lütgert, *Schöpfung und Offenbarung* (Gießen: Brunnen, 1984) 5–6.

Preface

It is an open secret. The doctrine of the divine attributes, both in dogmatics and in catechesis, has to this day been absolutely fruitless. In no locus of dogmatics has scholastic content been less willingly relinquished than here. Nowhere is the solution to problems sought more in the manner of formal scholastic analysis than here. Theologians ask if it is even possible to ascribe attributes to God! They wonder whether such attributes correspond to anything real in God, hoping by these devices to solve such problems as the concurrence of God's will and ability. They speak as if we still had some use for pagan ideas of "Pure Being" or "the Absolute"—shame compelling them to qualify their zeal for "the Absolute" by making it merely the first logical moment in their concept of God. They insist that, when it comes to speaking about God, any predicate must be strictly identified with its subject, God himself, so that certain divine attributes can only be known in their distinction from the world, while others are known only as we know their divine Subject. And so it comes to pass that the doctrine of the divine attributes has acquired the character of a muddle at best, a hodgepodge of *articulis mixtis* and *puris* in which, unfortunately, the *articuli puri* decrease as the *articuli mixti* increase. This sorry state of affairs explains the loose relationship between the doctrine of the divine attributes and other doctrines. It also explains why, of all the claims of dogmatics, those concerning the attributes resound least in the church's proclamation. The divine attributes arouse little interest in the congregation, particularly among those who express the deepest desire for the gospel and for knowledge of the truth. If the doctrine of the divine attributes is supposed to express an important aspect of the Christian knowledge of God, of the knowledge of God in his revelation, how is it that interest in it is confined almost exclusively to theological circles? Perhaps a merely academic presentation of Christian teaching on this point would suffice for a comparably academic understanding of God's action in his revelation and for guiding our expectations of him. But if this were so, why is it that this doctrine not only fails to resolve difficulties with the incarnation of Christ, but actually intensifies them? In fact, it so intensifies them that Thomasius thinks the Logos must relinquish certain divine attributes in the incarnation, while Ritschl and his school think that in the incarnation Christ must relinquish his essential divinity altogether. In circumstances like these, one can understand why Melanchthon would have to do today exactly what he did in that first edition of the *Loci*: just skip the attributes entirely. Slight have been the encouragements that this doctrine has given to Christian faith and knowledge, and seldom have they come. As one scans the series of claims that typically constitute this doctrine, one cannot help but ask, What is Christian in all this?

This is obviously not the way it is supposed to be. Claims made about God that do not stand in a direct relationship to our redemption are useless for faith and doctrine. And it is hardly an improvement to affirm such a relationship if one does so tediously, as the deferred outcome of a slowly linked chain of reasoning. The God who has revealed himself as love is and desires to be, for our sakes and in full fellowship with us, everything that he is. Therefore no claim about God can be valid if it does not bring this to the clearest and most effective expression possible. It is no doubt a good thing to point out that, when we say that "God is love," this love also bears the predicates of omnipotence and omnipresence and eternity. But this is still not to say everything that Ephesians 1:19–21, for example, says about the power of God, and so it ends up portraying our salvation as if it were not accomplished by *all* of God's attributes. But this is precisely what is necessary if it really is the *attributes* of God that we are dealing with.

A proper treatment of the doctrine of the divine attributes is only possible if we start from revelation itself, from the activity of God working through and in revelation, and exercising itself on us along with revelation to bring about our faith. For we know God only through his action for us and upon us. Our faith is evoked only by its object, by God himself in his action upon us. Therefore we can say nothing about God that we do not know objectively from his action and subjectively by the faith this action evokes, and so in such a way that the priority lies with God. Failure to attend to this is the charge that must routinely be brought against treatments of the divine attributes, even those of Albrecht Ritschl and Hermann Schultz. Let us therefore attempt, in accordance with the claim of revealed religion, to set forth the doctrine of the attributes of God as resulting from and at the same time further explaining revelation.

I

The Concept of the Divine Attributes

Christian faith will always find it bizarre to learn of the lengths to which the Greek fathers went, under the influence of Platonism, simply to determine whether or not God has attributes. The Scholastics took this question no less seriously, but their grand solutions have never in fact served to deepen Christian proclamation or make it more effective. One feels as if a curse has been lifted when one finally arrives at the first edition of Melanchthon's *Loci*, in which this entire question is boldly throttled and thrown overboard. But only too soon it climbs aboard again. In the subsequent editions of the *Loci* Melanchthon takes up this problem again and returns to the old questions. One can hardly claim that Melanchthon did so because his interests grew less religious and more formal and academic over time, or because he felt some need to keep his theology in dialog with philosophy. Bewildered, one begins to wonder whether it really is such a problem to ascribe attributes to God. Was not Quenstedt forced to admit that the attributes of God are "nothing other than inadequate concepts of the divine essence"? Did not Schleiermacher suggest that the attributes do not actually refer to anything particular in God, but only to particular modulations in our feeling of absolute dependence? If the claim that God has attributes creates such great difficulties, what is an academically minded theologian to do except make a *reservatio mentalis* every time Christian devotion and proclamation insist on speaking about God's attributes? One obviously cannot preach about a God who has no attributes.

Since the time of the Greek fathers, the concept of Pure Being, the Absolute, as applied to God, has made it seem impossible to ascribe attributes to God. Beyond this world of contingent and therefore definite and limited being, there lies Pure Being, the Absolute, the "really real," what Aristotle designated the Unmoved First Mover. Viewing God in this way is an attempt both to distinguish him from the world and also to interpret the world. We start by considering the world, we then remove all limitations from our thoughts about the world, and we think thereby to obtain a description of God. But the very attributes by which we then describe God lend him once again a definiteness and thereby a limitation that places him back among contingent and therefore limited beings. As a worldly being, God is once again limited in his capacity to act. In such a God one cannot believe. From such a God one cannot expect all things. Only an absolutely unlimited God can be believed in. And this was the religious interest of the fathers in the otherwise irreligious notion of Pure Being or the Absolute. This is why they either excluded or only partially accepted the idea that God has attributes. But they overlooked the fact that it is simply impossible to believe in the Absolute. It was only the fact that they identified this Absolute with the living God, the God revealed in Christ and recognized as free and powerful over all things—it was this identification that salvaged a concept that had never advanced the human spirit's quest for God but only thwarted it. Pure Being was the final thought of philosophy. The bridge from there to the world collapsed again and again every time it was dialectically reconstructed. The builders beheld in the gospel of Christ the mighty God of all things. He it was whom humanity had sought. It seemed to them as though God gave reality to the idea of Pure Being, which should after all be the cause of all things. But none of them asked whether it was right to preserve this concept of the Being of God alongside knowledge of the actual, living God. They treated both quantities as equivalents of the Aristotelian ideas of the Prime Mover and Pure Act. Mesmerized by this circle of thought, they were afraid to lose God again by attaching attributes to him, even though they could not help talking about righteousness, mercy, patience, etc.—divine attributes! But such talk, they reassured themselves, was only popular parlance.

Later theologians were concerned by a different issue. Speaking of God's attributes seems to require ascribing to him conflicting attributes, such as righteousness and mercy, as these are perceived and trusted in his action toward and self-manifestation to the world. As a result of this action, God's essence seems to acquire a new attribute, as a person acquires a new character or gifting in becoming a Christian. But faith relies on the essential immutability of God. On the other hand, it seems just as essential to maintain God's freedom to have acted otherwise. But if God's attributes are proper to his essence and not something in addition to it, the possibility of his having acted otherwise certainly seems excluded. And yet faith is inseparable from the confession that God can treat us differently than he does. He is not forced to act by some irresistible necessity, even if such necessity lay in himself. If God acted by necessity, there would be no sense in praying to him. In other words, the good must be good because God wills it; God does not will it because it is good. Still another concern appears in the Reformation and post-Reformation theologians. The attributes, says Quenstedt, do correspond to something real in God, but "our finite intellect cannot grasp, in a single concept, the infinite and most simple essence of God." Hence we use various individual forms of representation for the divine essence, but these forms appear to exist only improperly alongside each other.

Thus we find everywhere religious concerns for admitting into theology the philosophical denial that God has attributes, in both a strict and a limited sense. But this denial will always remain foreign to faith. We must therefore ask ourselves seriously whether academic theology ought to renounce the divine attributes, or more properly whether we theologians, for the sake of the divine attributes made known to us in revelation, ought to renounce our academic rights.

The faith that trusts in the grace of God, and praises the hallowed name of God, and hopes in the righteousness of God—such a faith can never renounce the divine attributes. But academic theology not only does not need the attributes; it cannot admit them at all. Academic theology need only recognize that, as with faith itself, so with the divine attributes it is dealing with an entirely different riddle than the one whose solution the old philosophy sought by thinking away the limitations of this world. Theology is not obliged to solve the riddles of contingent being or of nature. It was the attempt to do so that infinitely corrupted the theology of older and more recent times. Such riddles will actually solve themselves once we find a solution to that other and infinitely greater riddle, the actual riddle of the world: the riddle of history. If this greater riddle remains unsolved, the solution to every other riddle will be of no use. The ancient world had no interest in the riddle of history. Or, as far as it had any, it sought the solution via philosophical speculation, as if it were a riddle of nature—yet with none of the salutary awareness of its limitations that marks the natural sciences of today. Israel alone confronted the riddle of the world and gave it literary expression so profound as to tower over Greek tragedy itself. One need only recall Psalms 68 and 73 and the Book of Job.

The riddle of history does not consist in the conjunction of Spirit and Nature. It will not be solved either by discovering how Spirit stands out from Nature, or by finding a way for Spirit to maintain its independence from Nature. This way of phrasing the question only presents another form of the riddle of nature. But the riddle of history is this. How can there exist a world that in itself should perish? It should perish not because of its finitude and transience, but because of the law of sin and death ruling in it and thus the system of history that dominates it. This is the question that must torment not only the scholar and thinker but also the common person, who suffers under the law of sin and death and under that system of history determined by this law. This is the burning question for everyone, a question driven in the first instance not by a certain measure of education, but simply by a conscience whose voice has not been silenced. The riddle of history will not be solved by appeal to "reason in history," whose traces will at the very least not be perceived by everyone. The solution to this riddle must be intelligible to everyone if it is really going to be a solution. The same certainly cannot be said of the formulation of the riddle of nature and its answer—at least, not if Du Bois-Reymond is right to claim, "We do not know and we never will." The solution to the riddle of history, if it satisfies conscience and therefore reasoning, will also identify the purpose and goal of history and answer still further questions as well.

The hope of finding the solution to this riddle is the messianic hope of Israel. It is the Messiah's office to bring this solution. This is why both John the Baptist and Jesus proclaim, "The kingdom of God is near." That Jesus is the Messiah—this is the solution! This is redemption. Because Jesus is the Messiah, his community can wait patiently and with all confidence for the day when he will fully manifest himself to them. Until then, the community must be content with the firstfruits (Rom 8:23) and pledge of the Spirit (2 Cor 1:22). In this faith the messianic community awaits the Parousia and confesses of the one seated on the right hand of God the Father Almighty: "from thence he shall come to judge the quick and the dead." In the mission of Jesus the Messiah we have the self-manifestation of God to a world that is perishing in itself. In Christ we have the revelation of God that solves the riddle of the world, the riddle of history, not through explanation and instruction but through the self-manifestation of the essence, will, and power of God. The reality of God, in which he presents himself to faith, is a qualitatively different reality than that of Pure Being in its distinction from contingent being. It is the task of academic theology to recognize this difference, one that is far greater than that between nature and history. Theology cannot not let its task be set for it by the final thought of philosophy. Its task is not to explain the reality of God in terms of Pure Being or the Absolute or the world stripped of its limits, and certainly not to expand and modify this final thought so as to apply it to God. When the early apologists confronted the riddle of the world, they ought to have insisted on the right framing of the question and simultaneously provided its answer. But instead of pursuing so bold a tactic, they were content simply to identify that long-sought, final thought of philosophy with the God of revelation. This was fatal for theology. This is why "the oldest dogma in Christendom," the intensely cherished hope in the Parousia, which actually contains the solution to the riddle of the world, still exerted no influence on the apologists' negotiations with the cultured classes or on their academic presentation of the Christian knowledge of God. Had the dogmas of philosophy not exerted so dominant an influence, the hope in Messiah's return, to which the gospel directs our faith, would never have remained without influence on these tasks. As it was, the revelation of the reality of God was instead prostituted for the satisfaction of ancient intellectual desire. It was not until Augustine that the times grew wretched enough to require a new framing of the question. But when Augustine took up this question in *City of God*, the first work of the patristic era to address the actual riddle of the world, he had another aim and achieved another effect than a reconstruction of the doctrine of God. For centuries afterward, the leading lights in the history of western culture never fully sensed the ultimate incompatibility between the practical interest of faith in the revelation of God in Christ and the academic formulation of the doctrine of God. This realization was reserved for the era of the Reformation—admittedly, as we have seen, without achieving a decisive, sustained influence on theology.

Today we have no excuse to continue in these old ruts. We cannot do so once we have seen how great is the difference between the question that philosophy asks but can never answer and the question that revelation simply answers. We are directed to revelation, not as a last resort to obtain information that reason cannot find elsewhere, but because in revelation we have the reality of God. This reality shows us the right way to frame the question and at the same time gives us the answer. Revelation frees us from the compulsion of the futile ways of philosophy. In his revelation God acts. In revelation we come to know not the mere fact of God's existence—something acknowledged far too infrequently as it is. Rather, the self-manifestation of God, in which he is known as God, finally answers, or rather makes superfluous, the question whether he really exists. What we actually come to know in revelation is *who* God is and *what kind* of God he is. This is of a piece with the purpose of revelation: the accomplishment of redemption. Not the accomplishment of knowledge, but the accomplishment of salvation is the purpose of revelation. Concerning the purpose of revelation there still prevails a consensus among theologians, particularly since Karl Ludwig Nitzsch (1751–1831) and Karl Immanuel Nitzsch (1787–1868), even if opinions diverge widely about what revelation actually is. Revelation certainly results in knowledge, since God's revelatory action must obviously be known by those who encounter it. But this knowledge is only a means to the goal of redemption. God's revelatory action has a definite purpose: to manifest himself to our faith. But if God reveals himself without any attributes that can be known, without specific determinations of his will and power, then he cannot be believed in or even thought of at all. A God who cannot manifest himself to the world is not the living God. He is not God at all. The God who acts, who has purposes and accomplishes them, can no more do without attributes than his acts can. It is proper to God to manifest himself and to be his own redeeming manifestation, to distinguish himself as God, as the one to whose will, power, and action the world is absolutely bound. But if this is the case, then the attributes of his will and power made known in revelation are also the attributes of his essence. If in revelation God makes known how he exists and thus how he differs from all else that exists, it follows that his attributes indicate him uniquely, in such a way as to belong to him alone. These attributes do not limit him, they reveal him. They are thus attributes in the sense that their subject cannot exist at all without them. They are the predicates proper to God. None can be missing. Attributes that could be missing, or could be other than they are—attributes in the mere sense of *attributa accidentalia*—such attributes could not indicate God. Such attributes could only indicate how an individual is distinguished from its category, in the way that the natural sciences, for example, describe the objects of their attention.

We will only arrive at a more precise understanding of the attributes of God if we fix our eyes on the essence of God as it is made known in Christ. The essence of God is what makes God who he is for us: the Lord of all things, the source of life, our sole and everlasting support. Who God is for us—this alone, and not philosophical speculation about whether God exists, gives us knowledge of the essence of God. We thus draw a distinction between the concept of God and the essence of God. The concept of God, on the one hand, takes the term "God" not as a name but as a predicate. The subject who fits this predicate is understood to be the power that utterly transcends the world, to whose will and work the world is bound. In revelation, the Father of our Lord Jesus Christ designates himself as this power, the one to whom the world is absolutely, completely, and forever bound, the one who truly is God alone. Revelation does not tell us, however, how God exercises this power. Revelation does not identify the various conceivable possibilities of the exercise of this power, one of which ultimately, by the will of God, becomes reality. By revelation we know that it can be precisely and only this exercise of power through which he binds the world to himself. This alone is the highest exercise of power, not the highest that can be thought, but one that "our scanty thought surpasses far," one that we would not even expect, let alone be able logically to develop, if it were not actual reality. It is through this exercise of God's power that we first learn what it means for him to be God, in the rich and amazing meaning of this concept. The essence of God, on the other hand, is what must belong to God in order for him to be God. The essence of God is that through which he acts upon us and relates to us. We have no idea how it comes about that he exists. What we do know is that he is God. And so we also know how it comes about that we are bound to him and what this means for us.

Thus the essence of God corresponds to the reality of God made known in revelation, and it enables us to understand the characteristics of God's behavior and action. It is not enough, therefore, merely to claim with Nitzsch that God is "the eternal, personal Being of the Good," or with Herrmann that God is "the personal Will of the Good." While neither formula contains anything incorrect, each states only a partial truth, not the whole, and not even the really essential thing in God's revelation in Christ, namely, that it is precisely as he reveals himself in Christ that God is the reality of the Good. These formulas do not make clear that the Good is precisely and only what appears to us in Christ. We must therefore bind what we say about the essence of God firmly to his revelation in Christ. In revelation God appears and acts as the one who is entirely love, not merely one who has and feels love, but one who *is* love. He is and desires to be for us everything that he is, and he desires to have us for himself. He is the one who in love wholly opens himself to fellowship with us. He wants this. This is God's essence, the innermost being that fills him. It is as the loving God that he determines our being and our life. We know him and have him in no other way than in his love, in his active will to be ours, to belong to us as one person belongs to another. He does not want to be without us. That is the only reason we exist. That is why he has redeemed us. And that is why his action belongs to his essence, and why the determination of his action by his essence yields his attributes. In his attributes there appears the difference between God and us, upon whom he acts, in all of the connections posited by the fact of this relation. God's attributes are therefore his difference from us in all of the connections which his relationship with us brings, manifested for us and to us. They are the determination of his appearance in his action by his essence. The action and essence of God belong together in such a way that his action is the perfect operation of his essence. But if this is the case, then the attributes of God simply are the attributes of his essence. There is thus no basis, not even the possibility, for categorizing the attributes as either absolute or relative, internal or external, ontological or economic, transcendent or immanent. Such distinctions, even if merely conceptual, neither exalt nor deepen our knowledge of God. They are in fact more likely to obscure it. They make it practically impossible to maintain that it is the essence of God, indeed, the *entire* essence of God, that gives itself to us in revelation. If in revelation God gives himself entirely to us, and if he is therefore known by us as the one who is entirely for us, then there can be no aspect of God's being beyond his revelation, even though eternity itself will not suffice to exhaust all that he is for us. If God is everything that he is in his revelation, then no other attributes at all are appropriate to him, whether ontological or economic, than those we know in his revelation. It is especially because God's essence is wholly self-giving love that he acts out of his whole essence. This is true in all his conduct with us, and so in every attribute. In every attribute all the others are co-posited. There can be no question therefore of the sum of the attributes forming the essence of God. Such an opinion would testify to a total lack of understanding of the concept of the attributes of God. The attributes of God do *correspond* to the sum of the various aspects of God's relationship to us. But they do not themselves form a sum that *results* in the essence of God by way of addition.

They cannot do so, since none of them is anything particular in addition to the others. There can be as little a question of a sum of attributes as there can be of the possibility that one or another attribute might be missing, set aside, or inactive. We will see later that it is totally inappropriate to think of God as limiting himself in relation to human freedom, or indeed in relation to the effectiveness of any creaturely causality whatsoever. The attributes of God can be as little increased as decreased. They form a self-contained unity, which the religion of revelation has designated the glory of God. The attributes are, in their unity, the manifestation of the essence of God in its manifold activity—a manifestation that brings its object with it.

It is therefore of the greatest significance for the concept of the attributes of God that God reveals himself as love. If we have refused to designate God as "the eternal, personal Being of the Good," or as "the personal Will of the Good," this is because we do not know what the concept of the Good contains. It cannot be determined at the outset how far its content actually coincides with what we know from revelation as the essence of God, namely, love. From the revelation of God as love, however, we now recognize what the essence of the Good is. This frees us from the question—well-known but disastrously framed—whether something is good because God wills it, or whether God wills something because it is good. In the revelation of his essence as love, God shows himself to us as the one who desires to exist not for himself, but entirely for us. Yet it is not as if he needs us. Rather, this is his eternal, free self-determination. A self-determination to be nothing for oneself and everything for another is actually the most perfect self-affirmation. Such action is the most perfect self-actualization, the most perfect life, in which the subject joins his own being and life with determination and action for another, so that life leads to life, and life causes and creates life. Not to desire and act for others is not entirely to possess oneself. One only possesses oneself entirely, and thereby a fullness of life, when one determines oneself for the benefit of others. To refuse to give oneself to others is not to desire others, to desire no life beyond oneself, when in fact true life desires and strives after life. A life without others would be a life without purpose, without feeling or movement, a life good for nothing and no one, frozen in its indifference and inactivity, a dead life, a self-contradiction. To be completely for others is completely to live. Living belongs together with being for others. Being for others is thus at the same time both the purpose and the premise of life. Love therefore belongs to life, for only in love is life complete. Only in love is life a good both for the one who lives it and for those for whom it is lived. Love is thus the highest of goods and the highest good. For only that is good which is good for us and good for life. The good is thus the premise and the purpose of life. Love also is the premise and the purpose of life. Love is the Good. This insight fully stands the test when applied to us, to our purpose and task in life, to the question about the law of our life. The one through whom we exist, through whom we have a redeemed and eternal life because we have him, the one without whom we would not exist—he is the original and eternal reality of the Good, since he is life and love in one, and now brings about this Good also in us.

The knowledge that results from God's revelation in Christ, from the recognition of love as the essence of God and therefore of God himself as the original and eternal reality of the Good—it is this that allows us to understand revelation itself. Revelation is God's active opposition to that which ruins and destroys us, his opposition to sin and evil. That God does and must exercise this opposition lies in his essence. It lies in the fact that only the Good can have reality and permanence. God exercises this opposition in so wonderful and astounding a way because he wants to be what he is not against us, but for us. We are now at last in a position to fill out the content of the formal concept of the attributes of God that we have been dealing with thus far. The attributes of God are the determination of his appearance in his action through his essence of love. They are the determination of his appearance in his action in such a way that in his action the original and eternal reality of the Good is one with the movement toward the realization of the Good. It is in this way that God is the highest good and the highest of goods.

2

The Derivation and Classification
of the Attributes

From the start we must rule out any attempt to gather divine attributes according to the Areopagite's *via negationis, eminentiae,* and *causalitatis.* This is not, as Kahnis says, because such an attempt could well justify the most divergent concepts of God. The problem is that no knowledge of God can be gathered at all simply by magnifying our finite ideas—certainly not knowledge of the one who solves the riddle of nature, much less knowledge of the God who solves the actual riddle of the world, the riddle of history. We know God through his actual conduct, through his revelation, through his action for us and toward us, through the redemption that he offers to us. This is how we know the one who is God: we recognize him as he is God. We only know what it means to be God, or what the predicate "God" actually designates, when he himself brings about something so utterly unique that it could not be known from any other source than himself. Even having a sure conviction of God's existence, a conviction that makes itself felt in conscience and thereby presses on the intellect—this is still not knowledge of God, though it may lead one to seek God and perhaps feel one's way toward him and find him. To tread the path of the Areopagite would thus be to turn aside from the Christian knowledge of God. This is the case even when theologians take a knowledge of God properly derived elsewhere and inadvertently portray it as a result of the Areopagite's *viae,* whose actual function is merely (though very inadequately) to categorize this knowledge. We are bound to revelation and must derive our knowledge of God's attributes from it.

On the other hand, in deriving the divine attributes from revelation, we do not start with the being of God, as it is opened to us in revelation, and follow a logically compelling train of thought down to the attributes in which this being is expressed. Such derivation is not even possible with the objects of the natural sciences. Science must be content to understand the actual properties of its objects in connection with their nature, while still being unable to explain these objects fully. How much more does this hold for the knowledge of the God of revelation! The result of revelation, the knowledge of the being of God as love, is proof of this. For if love and loving behavior belong equally together, then the being of love—desiring to exist for others—rules out any thought of necessity. Least of all can we regard the actual revelation of the love with which we have to do as a necessary consequence of the fact that God is love, the original and eternal reality of the good that is directed toward the realization of the good. The revelation of love is indeed to be understood by love, but it is not to be construed by means of logical deduction. Love is the freest act that can be thought. One need only distinguish between loves. On the one hand, there is the love of natural attraction, of emotion, or love as a natural drive, a force to which we are more or less subject and in which we first desire others to exist for ourselves, before we desire ourselves to exist for others. On the other hand, there is the love that we know only if we have known God. This love desires to exist entirely and only for others. This love can overcome not only the absence of natural attraction, but even its opposition. In this highest, indeed actual, sense, to love means first and foremost to be entirely the master of oneself, mighty over oneself, and in the fullest sense free. This freedom of God's love is not even a "natural divine necessity," that is, it is not necessary for God even by any supposed law of his own nature. Recognition of this freedom is inseparable from the faith that is effected by God's revelation and joyfully receives his love. Such faith includes the inalienable certainty that God has no need of us. Even though God's entire, innermost being is eternally directed toward us, and even though we should never think of him otherwise than as existing entirely and eternally for us, it is nevertheless utterly by his own freedom—a freedom that is not mediated to him, not even through himself, and certainly not extorted from him through any necessity of reason or nature—that he desires to be for us and that we should therefore exist, so that love might have its object. The desire to grasp this conviction, and hold it ever and again before our eyes, is so natural to faith, so necessary, and belongs so intimately to faith's blessedness and peace that blessedness and peace are actually disturbed and destroyed, and faith itself weakened, to the extent that one allows the love of God to be interpreted as a necessity by appeal to the identity of freedom and necessity in the moral sphere—even if this occurs only in supposed connection to scholarly thought. It is certainly difficult to grasp conceptually the absolute freedom of the divine love, when precisely as love it desires an object. It seems that we should be able to say that such love *must* have an object, that it demands an object, simply because the concept requires an object. This difficulty only increases when we recognize that we are eternally the object of God's love. More precisely, God makes his being known to us as the one who eternally desires to be not just for anyone, not just for any possible object *in abstracto*, but entirely and only for us. It is an indisputable difficulty that this should appear to us precisely as freedom and not even notionally as necessity. But this should only prompt us to remain alert to the overwhelming reasons that compel us wholeheartedly to affirm, despite appearances to the contrary, the fact of this freedom in its paradox. To know God, one must be ready to affirm his transcendence over every law, whether moral, natural, or logical—a transcendence that nevertheless entails not the negation of law, but in fact the establishment of every law within the field of its validity.[1] For law is only valid for conditioned being, and not for the One who conditions all being, least of all for the One who so conditions all being as we see in the revelation of God in Christ. We actually have an analogy of this in our own life. When love says, "I must love!" the beloved cannot reply, "Yes, you must," but at most, "I must gratefully let myself be loved." But when the divine Love says, "I must love!"—as when Jesus saw Zacchaeus—it is hardly for us to speak of necessity. For the "must" spoken by our love is another matter entirely than the free "Must" of the divine love. The "must" of our love is necessary because it is the condition of our divinely ordained existence, and we are lost if we disregard it. We are obligated to the Love that obligates itself. But the self-obligation of God in no way places him in any state of obligation. We hold our life for the purpose, and therefore on the condition, that living and loving be united for us as well. But there can be no talk of conditions for the One who

---

1. With the development of the concept of the "supra-rational"—not a concept one would expect based on the revelation of God—what is said here cannot be disparaged as a renewing of the Scotist idea of the arbitrary will of God.

conditions all things. The limitation of the concepts of law and necessity to the sphere of created being and living is the first thing that we must never lose sight of.

The absolute freedom of the divine love presents itself to us in full clarity as it is revealed in Christ. If we hold this before our eyes, we will see how utterly impossible it is to derive from it, by some logical progression of thought, the particularity of its actions or attributes. For all of the attributes of God are strictly attributes of the love that is his being. The very fact of the divine love is the opposite of what has been found thus far by investigation into the scheme of things. One thinks of that expression of Aristotle, that the Divinity does not exist in order to love, but in order to be loved. But the love of which we speak, and the way in which it expresses itself, is far more than the mere opposite of all intended or actual results of investigation thus far. The action of the One who is love is precisely the opposite of *everything* that seems consistent with our thought or conscience, of all logical and moral consistency. It is the most wonderful activity of the transcendence of God over everything that is called law, whether a law of nature or of reason or of conscience, even over every "revealed law." This is transcendence not in the sense that it goes beyond everything that we could imagine without this revelation. Rather, even after it has been revealed, we recognize and experience it as the opposite of what we must ever and again acknowledge as logical consistency.

As Kaftan would have it, Christ's appearing is to be regarded "primarily from the viewpoint of the perfection of human development,"[2] rather than as the restoration of fallen humanity. If we had to view things in this way, then the transcendence of the love of God would admittedly be seen not in its opposition to every consistency of reason or conscience, but precisely in the magnificent and (considering our limitation) hardly imaginable consistency of its action. The opposition in which this transcendence of the divine love operates would be merely an opposition to the limitation and errors in our idea of God, to which we would have remained subject even without the revelation of love, and which we would now be obligated to renounce. The limitation of our thoughts and ideas about God is of course an indisputable fact. But this is not to say that the revelation of the love of God stands in opposition only to our *opinions* about consistency and not to actual consistency of reason or conscience. On the contrary, revelation

2. [Julius Kaftan, *Das Verhältnis des evangelischen Glaubens zur Logoslehre: Vortrag* (Freiburg: Mohr/Siebeck, 1896) 23.]

itself confirms not only the right of our good-conscience opinions about consistency. It even makes these a responsibility for us. It awakens and effects the recognition and acknowledgment of that which, in contrast to the revelation of love, would actually be consistent. The revelation of love in Christ demands and produces above all the kind of consistent moral thinking that we could not otherwise even attempt without despairing. Its goal, its content, and its significance are clear precisely to the one who allows himself to be compelled by it to consistent judgment. It is known as a divine act of boundless love in its opposition to what would actually be consistent. Hence its opposition to sin. The consistent action of God is suspected even beyond the realm of revealed religion, out in the heathen world where conscience reigns and compels people to witness against themselves and attest its liability to judgment. But as soon as God's revelation in Christ touches us and begins to deal with us and affect us, this self-offering of the divine love is immediately experienced as the strongest affirmation of the testimony of conscience to our actual liability to judgment, and at the same time as the opposite of consistent judgment. It also awakens this testimony of conscience right when it is has fallen silent. It obliges us, as we acknowledge our sin, ruthlessly to affirm our own condemnation, but also to recognize that the offer of grace is the opposite of all consistency. And to the degree that we misunderstand or forget grace's opposition to consistency, we will experience our faith as lifeless and impotent.

God's revelation in Christ, the revelation of redemption, cannot be understood as a matter of consistency, whether viewed from the perspective of the divine love or from that of human love and action. The former is even less possible in that the love that offers redemption in no way renounces judgment, but rather exercises it in a manner that transcends consistency. The very ones for whom love is intended actually contradict love's very essence when they see it from the perspective of consistency—a consistency they ought to have understood as grounded in love itself. This devaluing of love itself likewise devalues what love seeks to achieve. The love of God demands from those to whom it offers itself a consistent action that corresponds to it—the action of grateful, accepting faith. It is essential to faith that it regard the love of God as perfectly free and perfectly unconditioned—and certainly not conditioned by "God's goal for himself as it coincides with his goal for the world." Not even human love can be viewed from the perspective of consistency. But whatever contradicts faith contradicts the science of faith as well. If it wants to remain the science of faith, it is in no position to take any other perspective than that of faith, even secondarily, and repudiate such consistency with instinctive disgust in the interests of its uninjured self-preservation.

The love of God transcends the law of consistency. This is why it can redeem. But this transcendence does not consist in exchanging for our limited view of things some higher consistency that simply negates the law of consistency where it was thought to be valid. On the contrary, in devoting itself to our redemption, and thus refusing to hand us over to the law of consistency under which we suffer, the divine transcendence confirms that this law is in force and binding. The divine transcendence alone, and not we ourselves, is able to set us free from this law. It does not reveal to us that the sinner who sighs under the wrath of God is wrong to do so, for "whoever does not believe the Son, the wrath of God *remains* on him" (John 3:36). Only reflection that is sicklied o'er with the pale cast of thought would attempt to bind God's action to the law of scientific consistency in order to set a sinner free from receiving consistent treatment. Only such reflection could attempt to interpret the sighing of the sinner under the wrath of God as itself sin, or as the fault of a guilty conscience. The Christian knows this sin too, but as the sin of Cain, and not as the fault or even sin of seeking forgiveness and regarding as the wrath of God what is only his own sin. It is true that sin would result in judgment, if the sinner should remain in sin contrary to expectation and despite the revelation of love. This concession, however, fails to recognize that such a condition of being lost only obtains on the basis of redemption, but is not caused by redemption. Sin only needs this intensification in order to consign the sinner consistently to judgment. Only the revelation of redemption can completely open our eyes to sin. If this is so, it would not be consistent if we were to apply this recognition not to present sin and to the sinner as he finds himself before the love of God, but rather to future sin and to what can still become of it. The sinner *is* consistent as the love of God finds him and as he finds himself in its light: bound to judgment. The sinner not only *will be* forfeit to judgment, but is now forfeit to it and will henceforth remain forfeit to it, if he scorns the saving love offered to him. The appeal to the connection between sin and error changes matters all the less, if we recognize that even the sin of error requires not merely forgiveness. As Jesus himself attested on the cross, it requires *petition* for forgiveness, or rather *intercession* for forgiveness! For the sinner's petition must not be misconstrued as the form instinctively taken by acknowledgement of sin and the turning of the will from it.

God's revelation in Christ is consistent neither from God's standpoint nor in relation to our action. It is the complete opposite of all consistency. How then can one regard God's appearing "primarily from the viewpoint of the perfection of human development"? Introducing the idea of development, which generally corrupts the understanding of revealed religion at every step, does not misconstrue the actual current result of "development," whether in the history of all times up to the present or in the history of each individual. What it misconstrues is the riddle of the world brought about by revelation, by that particular action of the love of God, the riddle of history. How can there exist a world that is perishing in itself, and what will become of it? The essence of God's revelation in Christ is that God puts himself in opposition to this "development," a development from below, and not from above. As long as it remains the case that Christ himself has rightly understood and expressed both himself and his purpose, and does not, like others, need his self-awareness and self-testimony corrected by his epigones' understanding of history, so long will it remain the case that he came to seek and to save the lost, to call sinners and not the righteous. But so long, then, will it also remain the case that he did not come to make possible, at decisive points, the progression of "the history of development" to perfection. This is the great seriousness of the divine act of redemption, that the lost need no longer stay lost, and for this reason his responsibility is all the greater. Nevertheless and Notwithstanding: these are the hallmarks of the revelation of redemption, which only in this paradox creates belief and can be believed as the opposite of any and every form of consistency. Every attempt will be a fatal one—if only for scientific thinking—that undertakes to relieve this paradox and to put in its place the admirable grandeur and simplicity of the solution to the riddle of the world in terms of the consistent action of God, the knowledge of which should enable us henceforth to construct a scientific proof for the existence of God. Every attempt of this sort proceeds as if with inner necessity—if not for those who undertake it, then certainly for those upon whom they act—to underestimate God's opposition to sin and get entangled ever more tightly in the connection between the "the history of development" and its final outcome in the last day.

God's revelation remains in every respect the opposite of all rational and moral consistency. It is the revelation of the one who is never coerced by human sin into merely consistent action. This is the only reason we can believe in him and have hope. We must therefore utterly renounce the attempt at a consistent procedure for deriving divine attributes from the being of God. God transcends the law of consistency that is in force in the sphere of created being. The attempt would fail. Some have recently ascribed to the "theological speculation" of the prophets a quite significant contribution to the "development of revealed religion." But they fail to recognize that theological speculation has never yet discovered anything about God. Faith had this knowledge long before theological speculation discovered it, and faith has it as a gift from God, as revelation that produces faith, even the faith of the prophets. Faith proceeds not from discovery, but from revelation. And this revelation is conditioned not by any sort of progressive development but, as we see in the history of Israel and in the coming of Christ, by that divine rule that scorns all consistency: "Where sin increased, grace abounded all the more" (Rom 5:20).

We are therefore well advised to confine ourselves to revelation in our "derivation" of the divine attributes, so that we draw our assertions concerning the character of God's action exclusively from this action itself. This is the only scientifically permissible method. For attributes such as holiness that are only made known to us in revelation, the suitability of this method will be readily granted. But even outside the sphere of revealed religion, attributes of divinity are known, attributes that are implicit in the concept of divinity or in the predicate "God." The question is therefore whether, at least for such attributes as these, we ought to derive them from the concept of God. We would thus obtain a twofold series of attributes: one drawn from that concept of God shared by the heathen, for which we therefore have no need of revelation; the other known to us only through revelation. We would thus have returned to a twofold source for our knowledge of God and a mixed method for presenting it. But this would be to forget that even the predicate "God," even the concept of God, only receives its actual content from its subject, whose identity is his own, who acts in his revelation as "the one true God" and thus shows us what it means to be God. From the mere concept of God, apart from its subject, the Father of our Lord Jesus Christ, there results only entirely abstract assertions about omnipotence, omnipresence, etc.—assertions that each end in problems without offering solutions to any of them. We must therefore learn how properly to discern the omnipotence, omnipresence, omniscience, eternity, and immutability of the one who displays all of them in his revelation in Christ. This display, upon which alone our discernment depends, and upon which all further knowledge of God rests, cannot be understood at all as a logical inference from the idea of the power that is utterly superior to the world. Omnipotence, for example, like the concept of God itself, remains a strictly formal concept so long as one remains ignorant of who possesses it and how he exercises it. Only then does faith know what to expect from it. But such knowledge only comes from the actual activity of God in his revelation. We must therefore draw from revelation our understanding even of such attributes as these. In this way alone will we reach Christian knowledge, the Christian doctrine of the divine attributes.

This also means that our presentation cannot begin with the attributes that are implicit in the concept of God or the predicate "God." It is true for these attributes as well that every divine attribute is co-posited in all of the others, so that its expression, its manifestation, is materially determined through that which revelation alone discloses to us. It is thus essential to omnipotence, taking it again as an example, that it is the omnipotence of the holy God, or that it is the omnipotence of holy love. Our presentation must therefore begin with the attributes that are generally made known only in revelation. These will form the first series of attributes. There follow the attributes that are implicit in the divine predicate. These attributes, like the predicate of divinity itself, are materially determined and have their actuality only as the attributes of the God of revelation. Thus we obtain a second series: attributes implicit in the concept of God as seen in light of revelation. The suitability of this genetic procedure may be so obvious that it requires no critique of other methods, such as, for example, that of classifying the attributes as those of the divine being, those of the divine knowing, and those of the divine willing. H. Schultz makes a distinction between those attributes "known in creation and preservation," those "known in God's governing of the world," and finally those "revealed in his providence." But this distinction of various spheres for the manifestation of God's attributes contradicts the knowledge that in every attribute the others are co-posited, and it also contradicts the fact that in revelation God enacts and discloses his entire essence. We must for the same reasons avoid distinctions between ontological and economic, or transcendent and immanent attributes.

3

First Series

Divine Attributes Disclosed in Revelation

1. THE HOLINESS OF GOD

The revelation of God in Christ is the perfect revelation of his love. He is love for us, for sinners. This is so wonderful, so completely opposite to everything natural, to every rational or moral consistency, that not only is revelation required even to be able to imagine it, but more than that, something quite particular is required to be able to believe it. This particular is the experience that in revelation we are dealing with the perfect manifestation of God's opposition to sin, to our sin. In revelation, we experience this opposition. And in this opposition, God is known by us. Herein lies the binding and at the same time convincing power of his revelation. We see ourselves bound to bow before the one who allows us to feel this opposition, so that we must experience deep in our souls what he has against us, who is and wants to be entirely for us. But it is none other than merciful love that brings this about. We see ourselves justified, and not merely justified, but once again bound to believe in this love. It could only mean that we do not want to believe, if we seek to evade the experience of God's opposition to our sin. Not evading this experience, and yet still not losing heart, but trusting—this is the mark of Christian faith.

Judgment and grace are thus wondrously bound together in the revelation of God. And this not in such a way that the expression of grace only follows, once judgment has reached its goal, the goal of our conversion.

Neither does this mean we receive either grace or judgment, so that one and the same love responds in various ways according to our various conduct. The either-or before which love places us is either grace *and* judgment, or *only* judgment. This is how saving love in Christ encounters us. One cannot really believe in it, in good conscience, without opening oneself and giving oneself over to God's completely condemning opposition to our sins, an opposition that emanates from his person in love for sinners. Every half-measure, every lack, every reservation in this matter hinders faith. This opposition is already heard and found in his word; and what is found in his word, and strengthened through the impression of his person, is that he and he alone is the one "who knew no sin." The display of divine power and glory in his wonders forces from Peter's lips the only too understandable words, "Depart from me, Lord, for I am a sinful man!" The deepest, most piercing, and one might almost say annihilating experience, however, comes from the demonstration of his love, a love that forebears, suffers, intercedes, and dies that it may not abandon us but cry out, "Not lost!" From this love, from the cross of Christ, there flows out fully for the first time the power that allows us to experience what our sin is all about, thus uniting in itself judgment and grace. Judgment flows from grace. This is God's judging opposition to us and to our sin, by which we experience what God has against us. That this really is the case becomes clear if we recognize that the judgment ultimately carried out on the one who refuses to believe in this love is nothing other than what the believer, too, experiences, to whom this love has brought salvation, and what he continues to experience as "chastising grace." The difference is simply that the unbeliever wants to refuse and evade its judging force. For what he must ultimately experience is exactly what he now refuses to experience. This is why he rejects saving grace. Believers experience grace and judgment, judgment and grace, judgment through grace; the lost experience only judgment.

This unity of judgment and grace in the revelation of God in Christ is the perfect manifestation of God's opposition to sin, and it is precisely this opposition in which God is known and on which the binding power of his revelation rests. In our knowledge of God, this opposition comes first. Whoever refuses to recognize this will gain neither knowledge nor experience of the love that is the essence of God, whose first attribute is precisely this unity of judgment and grace. *This is the attribute of the holiness of God.* God's holiness is his active opposition to sin in the unity of judgment and grace.

We understand that this attribute of God can only be known where he enacts or reveals it. For it is simply not agreeable to the idea of God. It is just as unlikely to result from the development and nurture of the religious need we feel in our conscience. For this need, being a need for grace and forgiveness, can only be satisfied by a particular act of God. Thus we understand that, before God's revelation in Christ, Israel alone knew this attribute, for they alone knew the one who dealt with them as such. Israel alone spoke of the holiness of God—as did no one else.[1] Israel's religion is revealed religion in its pre-Christian stage, and as such the product—not the producer—of revelation. The fundamental characteristic of Israel's religion is consciousness of the holiness of God. It identifies itself as revealed religion by knowing, trusting, and hoping in the God whose goal in revelation is the display of his opposition to sin by means of saving love.

It is no evidence to the contrary to acknowledge that revelation in the Old Testament was not yet complete. Indeed, it was precisely the knowledge and experience of the holiness of God that grounded the hope of Israel in the complete manifestation of revelation in the messianic future. That is why "the Holy One of Israel" is the name to which Israel bound its hopes of redemption. This makes unlikely from the outset the claim of Diestel and Ritschl that, though the holiness of God is an essential idea of the Old Testament, it no longer corresponds to the New Testament's understanding of God. They argue that holiness in the New Testament seldom appears as a characteristic of God, and even then primarily in citations and reminiscences of the Old Testament. But this evidence is hardly compelling. Granted, other than in 1 Peter 1:16 (Lev 11:44; 19:2), Luke 1:49 (Pss 99:3; 111:9), and Revelation 4:8 (Isa 6:3), God is only called holy in John 17:11, 1 John 2:20, and Revelation 6:10, and this usage indeed has something strange about it at first. But this strangeness intensifies when we observe that "holy" is the typical predicate for the "Holy" Spirit, the Spirit whose "outpouring" is the actual fulfillment of the messianic promise, the messianic blessing itself (cf. Acts 1:4 with Luke 11:13; Matt 7:11; Rom 14:17). The innermost thoughts of God are present in the Holy Spirit (1 Cor 2:11). In the Spirit we have the saving presence of God on earth. The Spirit is active where God's salvation is proclaimed, so that we perceive God in no other way than as he deals with us in his word: as the God of salvation. It

---

1. For this and the following remarks I refer to the study of the biblical concept of holiness in my *Biblico-Theological Lexicon of New Testament Greek*, s.v. ἅγιος, and the literature cited there.

is by the Spirit that God's revelation in Christ is for us no mere fact of past history, but in the fullest sense present. By the Spirit the historic Christ is the living Christ present to us—not metaphorically but actually—Christ "the same yesterday, today, and forever" (Heb 13:8). It is the Spirit through whom and in whom all of God's revelation, even that of the Old Testament, is revelation in which God has not merely acted on our behalf, but is also experienced as the one who deals with us today. The Holy Spirit, the Spirit of the presence of God, is the one who brings about faith in us, the one by whom we become aware that in the word of proclamation God deals with us, and that God's dealing with us is the dealing of one who will not allow us to be lost, but has loved and loves us. He it is who convicts us of our sin and grants us forgiveness, who makes us aware of the guidance of God that has shaped our life in kindness and severity (Rom 11:22), who testifies to us that redemption is our own redemption, that Jesus Christ has come, that to have him is to have forgiveness of sins, that we are bound to Christ both now and forever, and that all who let themselves be bound to Christ through him, the Holy Spirit, are by grace children of God and with God. Since Pentecost, God has brought about his salvation in the world through the Holy Spirit, the Spirit of the appropriation of salvation. What we experience of God, we experience through him. He brings about repentance and faith, he offers us forgiveness and justification, he is the power of chastising grace, he is the one who obligates and enables us "to put to death the deeds of the flesh" (Rom 8:13), and it is by him that we cry, "Abba! Father!" (Rom 8:15), by him that we "grow strong in our inner being" (Eph 3:16), and by him alone that we can stand in temptation and overcome in trial. In short, *in him we experience God*—indeed, God in his redeeming love, God in the perfect manifestation of his opposition to sin. And the place where God is experienced in this way and whence the world should experience him is the community of those who are gathered through him into the community of God, the fellowship of his salvation, which is now a dwelling of God in the Spirit.

If this is the significance of the Holy Spirit, that in him we experience God, or the saving presence of God, it follows that the revelation of the Holy Spirit actually belongs not only to the old covenant, but appears in its entire fullness expressly in the new covenant. In the new covenant the innermost being of God becomes present and active in the Holy Spirit, thereby excluding any higher revelation. From this point forward we also understand that all of God's revelation is mediated through the Spirit of his holiness. This revelation identifies itself as God's as it displays his holiness, obliging us to recognize sin and giving rise to faith. In this regard it will both confirm the understanding we have reached and yield a more precise definition of the concept if we call to mind Old Testament revelation and the knowledge of the holiness of God that comes from it.

We cannot ascertain at what point Israel began to speak of the holiness of God. The only remnant of the oldest linguistic usage occurs in the designation of the temple servants consecrated to Astarte as קָדֵשׁ, קְדֵשָׁה. This speaks neither for (Delitzsch) nor against the supposition that this predicate was ascribed to the divinity even outside Israel. It depends on what the word means if we are to understand how Israel could fill it with the peculiar content of its unique knowledge of God. This meaning cannot be determined etymologically; it must be drawn from the use of the word. The first observation that suggests itself is that קָדוֹשׁ is the opposite of חֹל, of what is common. The idea of an opposition to what is common is basic to its meaning. A second observation immediately follows, that the word, with all of the derivatives of קדשׁ, is used only in a religious sense, and it denotes the same thing when applied to persons or things as when applied to God. Thus the opposition between קדושׁ and חל becomes an opposition between God himself or what is appropriate to deity and everything that is not associated with him. It is understandable that for Israel, who has YHWH alone to thank for its singling out from the peoples, קדוׁ became a predicate of God himself. God and Israel belong together. That is why Israel is holy and YHWH is holy. On this certainty rests Israel's religion, Israel's faith, and Israel's hope.

This makes it all the more important to inquire into the positive content of this idea. What is the nature of this opposition between God and Israel and everything that is חל? The observation that the opposition between קדושׁ and חל does not coincide with that between טָהוֹר and טָמֵא, but is related to it, does not bring us much further, because the opposition between pure and impure is used entirely in the cultic sphere. One has to accept that the requirement of purity, or rather the achievement of it, is intimately connected with cultic means of seeking and obtaining release from the miasma of guilt; with the basic idea of culminating worship in the priesthood or sacrifice in the place of "sanctuary," the dwelling of God among his people; and thus with moral purity. Thus the opposition that comes to expression in the predicate "holiness" is opposition to sin. Israel, singled out by God as a holy people, maintained their sense of belonging to God by maintaining the opposition to sin that this requires.

The same recognition can be achieved along different ways if we consider what it meant for Israel to be singled out from the peoples by the act of God. For Israel this meant release from the violence and injustice of its oppressors. For Israel, God's holiness was thus bound up with his display of opposition to sin and injustice, in a judging righteousness by which he rescues his people (Pss 145:17; 103:6). Thus for Israel the holiness of God stands in opposition to sin and injustice in general and so also within Israel itself. The sin under which Israel suffered and suffers must be kept at a distance if it is to keep its sense of belonging to God. The holiness of God is at the same time an obligation for Israel. It creates and requires holiness in Israel. It turns in judgment against Israel, whose sin provokes judgment. Isaiah 10:17: "The light of Israel will become a fire, and his Holy One a flame." It saves Israel, who devotes herself once again to her God, Isaiah 10:20: "The remnant of Israel and the survivors will lean upon the YHWH, the Holy One of Israel."

The holiness of God is thus bound up for Israel with the idea of being singled out, elected to be his people, as well as with the idea of everything that the holiness of God excludes from him and from Israel. That YHWH singled out Israel for himself, or the holiness displayed in this singling out, is and remains the hope of Israel. He is the Holy One of Israel, as Isaiah calls him (also 2 Kgs 19:22; Pss 71:22; 78:41; 89:18; Jer 50:29; 51:5; Ezek 39:7; Hab 1:12). As such, he is the Redeemer (Isa 41:14; 43:3,14; 47:4; 48:17; 49:7; 54:5,8), the Refuge for the lost (Isa 17:7–10), and on the day of redemption it will be said, "Great is the Holy One of Israel!" (Isa 12:6). But from the holiness of God proceed not only the election and rescue of Israel but also Israel's judgment. It will not allow Israel to perish, but neither will it allow Israel to go unpunished. Israel has profaned the name of God before the Gentiles by provoking his judgment, and it thus bears the blame for making it appear as if God were incapable of defending his people. And so God sanctifies his name once again before the Gentiles by rescuing Israel (Ezek 20:39–44; 28:22,25; 36:22–32; 37:26–28; 38:16; 39:7,21–24). It hardly needs to be said that we ought not conclude from this that "holy" is simply synonymous with "exalted, great, mighty" (Baudissin). For it is not power as such, but the way in which it is exercised that is the decisive consideration and that cannot be denied in Ezekiel. Israel's faith is thus expressed in trust, gratitude, and worship, as well as fear, while God's name is just

as profaned through unbelief as through disobedience, sin, and wrongdo-
ing: Pss 20:3; 77:13–20; Isa 65:25; Pss 106:47; 98:1; 102:20; 103:1; 105:3,42;
145:21; 22:4–5; Jonah 2:5–7; 2 Chron 30:27; 1 Chron 16:10; Pss 30:5; 97:12;
33:21 (we trust in his holy name); Isa 10:20; Num 27:14; Deut 32:51; Isa
29:23; 8:13; Exod 15:11; etc. The holiness of God is the fundamental and
formative principle of the covenant and thus of the religion of revelation.
It forms the lives of the people of Israel as it is expressed in the curses and
blessings of the law and in the ordering of worship around the expiation
that the law offers. It both requires and at the same time makes possible
the reconciliation that can happen nowhere else than in the dwelling place
and sanctuary of God (Lev 16:16–17,27,33; Num 8:19). The burning bush
that was not consumed (Exod 3:5) is its perfect symbol. The bush, which
is good for nothing except to be thrown into the fire, is Israel, who will be
not consumed but protected from the fire. The holiness of God demands
purification from sin, but also provides it, exposing sin but then covering it
and doing away with it (Isa 6). It only takes one offense to turn this sanctifying action of God into its opposite (Isa 10:17).

In this appears a majestic knowledge of God. Between God and the
world there is such an opposition that fellowship is only possible where
God separates and selects and makes a covenant with a people, yet without
ceasing to oppose sin. On the contrary, this opposition remains so intense
that fellowship with him is only possible through his free act of election.
Election is based on holiness. In the relationship established by election, it
is holiness from which forgiveness flows, so that God may be feared (Pss
103:1–13; 130:4). Only through forgiveness can the covenant continue.
That is why forgiveness is not merely included in God's founding act of
election, but must be sought again and again. When this is forgotten or
not observed, "the Holy One of Israel becomes a flame" and must judge
his people, so that they turn to him again, seek forgiveness, and find in the
Holy One of Israel their Redeemer. The religion of Israel—not as it was, but
as it was meant to be—rests upon this wondrous activity of the holiness of
God and upon the knowledge of sin that proceeds from it. This knowledge
of sin asserts itself in the religion of Israel and is asserted by the chosen
servants of God against Israel. And it cannot be denied that this knowledge
stands in indissoluble relationship with the knowledge of God in his revelation as the Holy One of Israel. The aim of all revelation, of all the proclamation and manifestation of God, both in his guiding of Israel and through
his servants, the prophets, is to bring Israel to a knowledge of its sin and his

holiness, so that it gets serious about religion in its life. Not all revelation takes place in relation to an ascending development of Israel's religion. A history of the religion of Israel, which assertions of such development seek to portray, is unhistorical and scientifically untenable. For it contradicts reality not despite but because of this idea of development. Revelation is the activity of the holiness of God according to a single principle: "Where sin increased, grace abounded all the more" (Rom 5:20)—until at least Israel's constant turning aside to other gods is finally brought to an end. But immediately there begins a new straying, one that ultimately culminates in the rejection of Jesus.

It is therefore not even half right when Quenstedt claims that the holiness of God is "that highest purity in God, completely and utterly free from every blemish or defect, which requires of all creatures cleanliness and due purity," and that God, because he is the highest good, shows himself to be holy "by proclaiming and upholding the highest good through the moral law." The restriction of God's holiness to the moral law makes the claim even less correct. For it is not in the moral law but in the cultic that God's holy counteracting of sin found its actual statutory expression. But above all, this claim completely overlooks the fact that God's holiness is first and fundamentally experienced in the election and guiding of Israel. These are the ways that God shows himself to be, both in grace and in judgment, Israel's God and Redeemer. The law is not the actual revelation of holiness. It is only the means by which the people are kept in fellowship with God. First and foremost there stands the singling out, the election of Israel, God's covenant with Israel, and God's self-obligation to this covenant and his self-manifestation within it. So the holiness of God experienced and believed by Israel extends far beyond the law. Holiness is the New Testament element in the revelation of the old covenant. The holiness of God, both as Israel experienced it and as the basis and content of Israel's faith and hope, is God's wondrous opposition to sin, displayed in grace and judgment toward and within Israel, by which Israel anticipated the future in which it hoped.

There is certainly something right in Ritschl's claim that God's holiness in the Old Testament expresses something of the incompleteness of revelation at that point. Utterly wrong, however, is what Ritschl means by this, namely, that in the New Testament revelation something else takes the place of God's holiness. No, the New Testament revelation is exactly what Israel should have expected from God's holiness. The New Testament is the completed revelation of God's holiness, the manifestation of his opposition to sin in that wondrous unity of judgment and grace, in which God's counteracting of sin is accomplished. A new and higher revelation, a further advance of Christianity, a richer and deeper knowledge of God there could never be.

God's exclusive opposition to sin and to the sinful world—for sin inheres in a subject—cannot be brought to sharper expression than by the fact that fellowship with God is only possible if he, of his own accord, in a free act of love chooses someone. There can be no more complete condemnation of sin, nor any stronger counteraction of sin so as to break its dominion, than that which God himself and he alone makes possible for us in his electing love, so that we may no longer serve sin but remain in fellowship with him and live for him. If this is a fact—and it is—then any other possibility of rescue from the ban and curse of sin is ruled out, and the idea of development is finally set aside. It is wrong to see Israel's belief in its election as an expression of Old Testament particularism, which the New Testament replaces with the universalism of grace. Election remains in the new covenant—assuming it reflects reality to say, "It does not depend on human will or exertion, but on God's mercy" (Rom 9:16). Love is known as freely choosing its object, and thus as holy, in the sending, the appearance, the conduct, and the life and experience of Christ and in the work of the Holy Spirit conforming us to salvation. This revelation and activity of the world-embracing love of God is experienced as the opposite of all consistent execution of his opposition to the world and its sin, to us and our sin, and nevertheless as the perfect execution of this opposition. And our conscience condemns it. Love is experienced by each individual as free election that stands in total opposition to his previous development, just as it shares itself with him in inconceivable distinction from others. No one ever "developed" into a child of God. The Gentiles, in distinction from Israel and in the place of Israel, and the individual in distinction from others, experience and confirm that the divine will to salvation takes place according to election.

God's holy action brings about both the correct knowledge of sin as well as faith. It thus confronts the whole of paganism, whose basic features are fear and anxiety, by requiring us to trust in God. We would never dare to do this if we only considered that such trust brings with it an unavoidable submission to judgment. But the wondrous action of God's total opposition to sin, in the unity of judgment and grace, is that he himself brings about this trust in us, in a way that clearly transcends any law of rational and moral consistency. This is how God dealt with Israel in its history, in the men he gave to it and in instituting its law, and ultimately in sending Christ. This divine action comes to completion in us through the working of the Holy Spirit, who spoke from above the word concerning everything that God has done for us and is for us, and who is experienced not as absent, but as the presence of God and as the free gift of his electing love, a gift that is neither bound to nor conditioned by anything. In this way faith comes to know that we, as sinners, can trust in God precisely because he stands in this opposition to sin. When the disciples ask the question, "Who then can be saved?" it is only because Christ is the Holy One that can give the answer that otherwise would have been sought in vain: "What is impossible for man is possible for God, for nothing is impossible for God" (Matt 19:25–26).

Through the revelation of the holiness of God, we see for the first time the actual divinity of God. His holiness shows us the fact that he is God, and the way in which he is God, the way he reigns as the power absolutely superior to the world. He is this power, he alone is God, because he alone, as the Holy One, holds in his hand and dispenses the solution to the actual riddle of the world, the solution to the riddle of history, the history both of the entire world and of each individual. How can a world exist, how can a person exist, and what will become of them, of each individual and of all of them, when in themselves they are perishing under the law of sin and death that oppresses them? Answer: not through development, but only through the counteraction that flows from the holiness of God, in the unity of judgment and grace, in the display of electing love. The power of revelation lies in its holiness, which obliges us to believe and also enables us to do so. Holiness is the decisive attribute for knowing and recognizing God, and for understanding his will and his ways. All further knowledge of the attributes of God depends on holiness. If we do not recognize or understand God's holiness, we will never comprehend his deeds and actions.

2. THE RIGHTEOUSNESS OF GOD

Where God reveals himself as the Holy One, there he will also be known as a judge. That is why the idea of his righteousness or justice is undeniably bound to the idea of his holiness. He is the judge of all the world, who lets it experience that there is salvation only for those whom he chooses in free love, and so salvation only by grace through the One who—instead of eternally excluding us and denying himself to us—offers himself to us in electing and redeeming love. That is why the awareness of responsibility is so tightly bound together with the faith that he brings about in us. Faith becomes impotent and lifeless to the degree that this awareness fades. No one can have any such idea of God's judgment except the one who "has received mercy," or who feels himself bound to say with Paul, "It does not depend on human will or exertion, but on God's mercy" (Rom 9:16). There is not the least inconsistency with the full, New Testament knowledge of God, no remnant of an earlier or sub-Christian notion, when 1 Peter 1:17 says, "If you call on him as Father, who judges each one impartially according to his deeds, conduct yourselves with fear throughout the time of your exile." Or still more strongly, Philippians 2:12–13: "Work out your salvation with fear and trembling, for it is God who works in you, both to will and to work." There is no faith in the Fatherhood of God, in our election and redemption, that does not bind itself to an unqualified recognition of God as judge.

This faith is another matter than the awareness of judgment that asserts itself in conscience even apart from revelation. Conscience compels not only us, who stand under the influence of revelation, but—as Paul says and as all the missionary work of our century confirms—all the heathen as well, to acknowledge their own liability to judgment. The effect is fear, nothing but fear and anxiety, the fear that is the basis of all heathen religion. Completely different are the awareness of responsibility and the belief in God's judgment that are established in the faith that comes from revelation. What we must take responsibility for in judgment is this: whether we have what has been given to us. We are responsible for our state of salvation. The rule that applies to us in the judgment we await is: "To everyone who has, more will be given; but from the one who does not have, even what he has will be taken away" (Matt 25:29). For God not only gives what he requires, but also requires what he has given. Those upon whom the electing and redeeming love of God has come to rest, and in whom it has brought about faith, *have already experienced God as judge in the grace they have received.* For them, future judgment means that, in distinction from the world out of which they were chosen, their just cause will be brought to light, and they will receive justice against those who do them injustice or who are unjust, and who thus have received the grace of God in vain.

But where God is experienced as judge, there his judging righteousness is experienced. For his judgment is a judgment in righteousness, and where he shows grace, there he forgives sin. Indeed, it is precisely this that must be regarded as the highest proof of his judging righteousness, rather than, by our way of looking at things, the opposite of righteousness. For God cannot act more decisively as judge than when he shows that he has power to forgive sins and that there is no other salvation than what he brings through forgiveness. It is not a salvation *from* his hand, but a salvation *through* his hand. Either he ceases entirely to be a judge—and not only for those he forgives—or he forgives as judge and therefore in righteousness, "so as to be just and the one who justifies the ungodly" (Rom 3:26; 4:5), whereas the law says, "you do not justify the ungodly" (Exod 23:7).

Here it becomes apparent how and why righteousness, like holiness, is an attribute of God, of which one can have no idea apart from revealed religion. As in his holiness, and tightly bound up with it, God shows himself exalted in righteousness over the law of rational and moral consistency, yet without abolishing this law. For there can be no stronger affirmation of the moral law than the forgiveness that binds sinners to God's judgment. Again, there can be no greater opposition to all lawful consistency, no more complete exemption from the law, than the forgiveness of God in freely electing love. From what point of view, then, are we to consider forgiveness, the display of grace, as the action of the judging righteousness of God? If our explanation is right so far, we cannot accept an opposition between righteousness and grace that requires adjustment whenever God shows grace. For it is in showing grace that God is experienced as judge and as righteous. We recall here what Karl Immanuel Nitzsch says about setting righteousness and love against each other: "To attribute to God some other basic intention beside and apart from love—this is nonsense."[2]

The problem that lies before us has been often seen but never solved. This is because we have grown accustomed to a regrettable theological and practical tradition. For it is no solution when Friedrich Nitzsch, following the example of the Socinians and to some extent that of Johann Gerhard as well, appeals to the mediating concept of "equity" in order to explain the application of the concept of righteousness to God's saving and gracious acts. According to Aristotle, equity (*epieikeia, Eth. nic.* 5.10) is "the gentleness of the judge who, without violating the law or showing partiality, takes individual circumstances into consideration."[3] God, therefore, "in consideration of the particular need for protection of his faithful covenant

2. [K. I. Nitzsch, *System der christlichen Lehre*, 6th ed. (Bonn, 1851) 178.]
3. [F. Nitzsch, *Lehrbuch der evangelischen Dogmatik* (Freiburg, 1892) 419.]

people, and as a *gentle* judge and sovereign, manages the prevailing standard of righteousness that flows from his own holiness in such a way that it is not 'an eye for an eye' but grace that prevails." But such grace is no longer real. It is merely the restraint in God's display of righteousness. It dispenses with law rather than affirming it, and it contradicts that election whose very essence is the exclusion of all such considerations. Neither is it any solution when Ritschl identifies the essence of God's righteousness not in the exercise of judgment, but defines it instead as "his self-consistent and undeviating action that is consistent with the salvation of the members of his community; in essence it is identical with his grace."[4] This definition does not become right simply because God's action is described as "consistent with" salvation rather than "appropriate to the goal of" salvation—as if this kept it somewhat true to the supposed etymologically basic idea of the Hebrew word and avoided the appearance of confusion with the concept of the divine wisdom.[5] Following Leibniz's definition of righteousness as kindness directed by wisdom, Hermann Schultz explains righteousness as omniscience determined by holiness, where God's omniscience is understood as being the omnipotence of the divine end in itself, which God actualizes without any conditions, means, or limitations outside of himself. But in this way the concept of the righteousness of God acquires a content that in and of itself has nothing to do with God's judging action and only makes such action comprehensible under circumstances that immediately have nothing more to do with grace. But this contradicts the way in which we come to know this righteousness. If our knowledge of both God's righteousness and holiness comes about as we perceive in revelation how he opposes our sin and obliges us to believe, and especially if our knowledge of his righteousness arises as we experience him as judge in this obligating power, then we cannot seek a solution to the problem by using a definition that essentially excludes the problem and then introducing new terminology.

Both theology and church life have inherited an understanding of righteousness as an abstract law, muddled such as it is, of so-called distributive justice. Ritschl objects that such a concept does not derive from revelation, but has its roots in antiquity, and he is partly right. But his objection applies all the more to his own understanding, as well as to most

4. [Albrecht Ritschl, *The Christian Doctrine of Justification and Reconciliation*, trans. H. R. Mackintosh and A. B. Macaulay (Edinburgh, 1900) 3:473–74.]

5. Cf. Ritschl, "Geschichtliche Studien zur christlichen Lehre von Gott," in *Gesammelte Aufsätze* (Freiburg, 1896) 2:168: "God's action is righteous in that it orders the means to the end of the kingdom of God among people."

attempts—e.g., those of Philippi, Frank, and Dorner among others—to give to the concept of righteousness a broader sense than that of the judging action of God's power. The only difference is that any interpretation of religious ideas that hearkens back to an ethical concept of righteousness as the highest virtue, one that determines and comprehends one's total moral conduct, must itself grow from the same roots that have nourished both the medieval interpretation of justification an infusion of righteousness as well as all modern attempts at an alleged deepening of the doctrine of justification. This will always be the case where righteousness is bound up with the idea of a highest standard of conduct, whether this standard is a highest and ultimate goal of conduct or the idea of the good as the supreme law.

By contrast, it is absolutely right to see a strong connection between God's righteousness and divine judgment. It is only wrong if this judgment comes to be seen one-sidedly as punishment. This is the mistake that is rooted in antiquity, and even then only in a qualified sense. For one does not speak of the "righteousness" or "justice" of the divinity or of the gods when they are seen as judges and avengers of injustice, or when one expects from their dominion less a reward for good than punishment for evil. Plutarch, in his *On the Delays of the Divine Vengeance*, tried to preserve his faith in these gods despite his constant trembling before the grim reality of the course of this world. Even if one endeavored in all seriousness to ground this dominion of the gods—more wished and hoped for than believed—on some idea of their righteousness or justice, and only in this sense to ascribe to them the predicate "righteous" or "just," one would always remain far from Greek and Roman thought. But how could antiquity have thought even this much? For though they did believe that there were gods and did ascribe to them specific functions, they never spoke of this belief as trust, as they would have had to do in order to ascribe to the gods justice, that highest of Greek virtues! This could not happen where one only had to make the gods propitious if one sought their beneficence.[6]

It is not from antiquity that we derive the explanation of the punitive dominion of God as righteousness, or the relation of the righteousness of God one-sidedly to this punishment. These are connected to this day with sin, with the fact that the power of revelation that demands faith lies in

---

6. Leopold Schmidt, *Die Ethik der alten Griechen* (Berlin, 1882) 1:47ff. Karl-Friedrich von Nägelsbach, *Homerische Theologie*, 3rd ed., rev. Georg Autenrieth (Nuremberg, 1884) 320ff.; Nägelsbach, *Nachhomerische Theologie* (Nuremberg, 1857) 28ff, 345ff. Schlatter, *Der Glaube im Neuen Testament*, 1st ed. (Leiden, 1885) 69ff. See my *Lexicon*, s.v. δίκαιος, ἱλάσκεσθαι, πίστις.

God's opposition to our sin, which we perceive in revelation and through which revelation has its effect upon us. It is understandable that the working of the Holy Spirit was first experienced as conviction (ἐλέγχειν), awakening conscience as a consciousness of guilt and a certainty of being liable to judgment. The fact that God offers faith to everyone and also "commands all people everywhere to repent because he has fixed a day on which he will judge the world in righteousness" (Acts 17:30–31), was likewise first experienced as demand and command before it was understood as gift and grant. At the same time, this is the complete opposite of all rational and moral consistency—as if it were at all a simple matter to find consistency in the unity of judgment and grace. With the entrance of the Germanic peoples into the church, the gathering of voluntary communities was eventually replaced by established churches, and the catechumenate by preparation for confession. Drawing on the educational practices of the ancient world, classical ethics was Christianized through the simple addition of three theological virtues to the four ancient cardinal virtues, so that Christianity came to be seen almost entirely as a new law. It was almost inevitable in these circumstances that the phenomenon would recur in the church that we saw in the Jewish synagogue. Israel expected redemption through the judgment of the saving righteousness of God. But this hope changed into fear. If this redeeming judgment was understood to be punishment for Israel's oppressors, one could no longer imagine judgment even upon Israel as anything but punishment. In this way the law, and through the law sin itself, became too powerful. Even the prophecy had said: "In the city that is called by my name I begin to work disaster" (Jer 25:29). There was no longer an answer to the question, "How can a sinner be or become righteous, or present a righteous case before God, so that God will intervene for him in judgment?" Such righteousness was sought but not found. In 4 Ezra, hope still clung to the possibility, which even then was only sensed from afar, of an unexpectedly favorable outcome in judgment. For a long time there was no admitting what Paul first admitted in Romans 7 and unreservedly confessed on the basis and as a result of his conversion, since he no longer needed to hide it. The author of 4 Ezra only admitted it when forced to do so by the brutality of history, the destruction of Jerusalem by the Romans. Then only do we find it expressed by a Jew, because he was then obliged to adapt this realization to his system of thought in order to maintain himself.[7] This is the same concept of the righteousness

---

7. Lütgert, *Das Reich Gottes in den synoptischen Evangelien* (Gütersloh, 1895) 39.

of God that dominated the theology and practice of the medieval church and still dominates the Roman church today. It thus gives unwilling testimony to the fundamental significance of a right understanding, which we must seek. It lacks an understanding of the unity of law and promise, and so also of the fulfillment of both in God's revelation in Christ. Through the law comes the knowledge of sin, "so that every mouth may be stopped, and the whole world may be held accountable to God" (Rom 3:19). But we are not eager to affirm this knowledge, and it is only against our desire that the confession of it comes to our lips, "for they were ignorant of the righteousness of God" (Rom 10:3). Israel lost its understanding of the actual content and goal of revelation, and the medieval church did not find it. Thus the religion of the synagogue acquired a sub-Israelite character, and that of the medieval and Roman church a sub-Christian character. This is the one right aspect of the claim that this concept of righteousness as a punishing righteousness derives from Greek thought. It has an ethnic character. Only by clinging to the one true God can we resist being drawn into paganism.

It is all the more strange that even Protestant orthodoxy stood fast by this concept of righteousness. Flacius himself chose a better path when he explained the righteousness of God as "God's kind liberation of us from our oppressors and his vindication of us." He adds: "It is said of God that he leads out our righteousness and brings it into the light, when he sets free from difficulties our righteous cause and us ourselves, gives us victory, and thereby sets up a witness of our innocence and righteousness before all the world; cf. Jer 51:10" (*Clavis scripturae sacrae*, s.v. *justitia*). The theologians, however, did not follow this path that led to the gospel of justification by faith and to the God who is "just and the justifier of the one who has faith" (Rom 3:25). Johann Gerhard cites with wholehearted approval a line from Gerson: "When God wants to show mercy, no one is gentler; when he wants to show righteousness, no one is more terrifying." Gerhard sees the significance of this divine attribute in that it "can call back the wrongdoer from abusing God's goodness." Opposition against abuse of the gospel, against the "antinomians and law-stormers" (Luther, *EA* 58.336), is thus the reason for the emphasis on righteousness as a punishing righteousness. The theologians did not actually limit righteousness to punishment, but understood it as "the highest and unchanging divine rectitude that demands from the rational creature what is right and just" (Quenstedt), or as "an active divine attribute, the power by which God wills and achieves all things that are in conformity with his eternal law, and by which he prescribes appropriate laws for creatures, rewards the good, and punishes the wicked" (Hollaz), thus capitulating entirely along the lines of the Greek idea of justice as the highest virtue. But precisely in doing so it once again became impossible to think of the human experience of the righteousness of God other than in the form of a punishing righteousness. God's righteousness demands human righteousness, does not find it, and must therefore punish. Only hypothetically can there be any talk of reward. In reality no one is to be rewarded. There was only one who could have been entitled to a reward. But despite this, Christ took upon himself, in our place, the punishing righteousness of God, so that grace might reign over us. In this connection of ideas, there is no place for a righteousness of God that would be the hope of sinners. Luther once explained: "Long ago, that expression, 'the righteousness of God,' was like a thunderbolt in my heart. For when I was under the papacy, I read, 'save me in your righteousness' (Pss 31:2; 71:2), or 'save me in your truth.' From that moment on I thought that righteousness was the fierce wrath of God by which he punishes sin. When I read that the righteousness of God is revealed in the gospel, I hated St. Paul with all my heart. But afterward, when I noticed the context and what follows, 'As it is written: "The righteous lives from his faith,"' and when I also read what Augustine said about this passage, then I rejoiced. For I learned and saw that God's righteousness is his mercy, by which he considers and deems us righteous."[8] God's mercy is righteousness, and God's righteousness is mercy. How infrequently this is recognized may be seen in Johann Gerhard's embarrassment when he notes in passing the fact that "the word 'righteousness' is often understood as goodness." The only other thing he knows to say is, "It appears to mean that it is righteous, and in accord with the nature of God, to show goodness to the miserable and to those who implore his help." We have here, if not exactly, then almost that Socinian idea of equity so vigorously repudiated by Gerhard. He begins with righteousness as the perfect virtue, and from there proceeds to the perfect fulfillment of duty in every position and calling: "But who conducts himself in his position and office so well and perfectly as God? Every aspect of his office, so to speak, he administers righteously and in every way perfectly. He is a righteous Lord, a righteous judge, a righteous father, a righteous king, a righteous teacher, a righteous spouse, a righteous lawgiver." To this righteousness belongs distributive justice as well as the corrective justice that "corrects mistakes without regard for persons and punishes the perpetrator of harm." Beyond these Gerhard

8. [Cf. *Luther's Works* 54:308–9.]

also knows of a promissory justice, "which is nothing else than truthfulness and trustworthiness in what is said or promised," and so here as well we have nothing else than a highest virtue—with no thought that even in the fulfilling of promises the judging righteousness of God could be known. On the contrary, even promissory justice only serves to intensify terror before judging righteousness or distributive justice, as Gerhard's appeal to (Pseudo-)Augustine shows: "The one who is true in promising is also true in threatening" (*De vera et falsa poenitentia* 7.18). That one need not perish in this terror before the judging righteousness of God, and that religion could be better than theology, is no thanks to this understanding of God's righteousness. We owe thanks, rather, to the recognition reclaimed by the Reformation that there is a human righteousness that is otherwise disposed than the δικαιοσύνη of the Greeks and Scholastics, one that flows from God and is therefore called after him δικαιοσύνη θεοῦ, the righteousness of God, whose subject is the believing sinner. What remained unrecognized was that the judging, active righteousness of God, enacted and displayed in revelation, could itself bring about a trusting faith.

This is really not so hard to understand, if only one can first get free of the influence of the Greek idea of δικαιοσύνη as the sum of all virtues, which is to be found even in the beloved explanation of the idea as "uprightness." We must direct ourselves to where we got the idea of the righteousness of God, to the testimony of revealed religion that lies before us in Holy Scripture. We know that revealed religion even in Israel, as likewise in Christianity, was never an established religion in the sense that the entire people actually lived it out in full seriousness. Even in Israel it was always and only the possession of the few who took it seriously. It was not even the possession of those who were considered and considered themselves the virtuosos and official representatives of religion. It was the property and possession and life of "the quiet in the land." Holy Scripture of the Old and New Testaments gives us a clear view into both: both what the religion of Israel was, and what it was meant to be—and this is not its least impressive validation as a reliable document of revealed religion.

But then there is the fact that the whole of Scripture reckons with the idea of the judging righteousness of God, and only with such righteousness. Even the saving righteousness to which the promise points and from which Israel hoped for redemption is itself judging righteousness, and this despite the fact that Israel prays with the psalmist, "Enter not into judgment with your servant, for no one living is righteous before you" (Ps 143:2). This awareness is so decisive that Karl Immanuel Nitzsch says: "As is generally known, in the midst of the covenant of grace both reward and punishment maintain their validity, and so therefore does the whole idea of retribution. It is not to be doubted that this idea is the substance of righteousness."[9] The sub-Israelite tendency mentioned above reckons with the same idea, because it expected salvation only from the judging righteousness of God, even though it could still only fear this righteousness and no longer dared in faith to hope in it. This is precisely what shows the fundamental significance of this awareness for the religion of Israel.

The prophets announced the redemption of Israel as an act of the righteousness of God, and this redemption was expected, desired, and requested by Israel an act of the divine righteousness. All trust in God was a trust in his judging and therefore saving righteousness. This is all so clear as day that it hardly needs a detailed proof. We need only recall here the well-known connection between the righteousness of God and the salvation of God (Isa 56:1; 45:8,21; 46:13; 51:5–8; 59:17; Pss 65:5; 51:14; 112:4; 116:5; 31:1; 36:10; 98:1–2; 103:17). In Micah 6:5, the acts of God that he showed Israel in the redemption from Egypt are called "the righteous acts of YHWH."[10] Everywhere that the righteousness of God appears as bringing salvation, it is thought of as a judging righteousness, which brings justice to afflicted Israel and so brings an end to its affliction. Micah 7:9: "Because I have sinned against him, I will bear the indignation of YHWH, until he settles my case and establishes justice for me. He will bring me into the light, and I will look upon his righteousness." That is why the promise proclaims the year of redemption as a year of retribution, to set things right for Israel (Isa 34:8; 35:4; 61:2; Hab 3:12–13; Hag 2:22–23; Zeph 2:8–11; Zech 14; Mal 4; Ps 58:10–11). For the goal of judgment, and of the exercise of righteousness in judgment—and this is the basis of this idea—is to help those who need justice to obtain it. The relief that the violated and oppressed need, those over whom injustice prevails, is to find a judge who will look after their rights. The judge and his righteousness is chiefly for those who are otherwise treated as having no rights on earth, those whose "fence is low," for the widows and orphans, the poor and the weak. Thus Isaiah 11:1–4 says, "The shoot from the root of Jesse will not judge by appearances, nor

---

9. K. I. Nitzsch, *System der christlichen Lehre*, 6th ed., 179.

10. For what follows, see the detailed examination of the entire biblical usage in my *Lexicon*, s.v. δίκαιος κ.τ.λ., as well as βασιλεύς, βασιλεία, κρίνειν, ποιμήν, πραΰς, πτωχός, ῥύειν, σώζειν, and my forthcoming study of the Pauline doctrine of justification.

render judgment by what his ears hear. With righteousness he will judge the poor and bring justice according to law to the miserable of the land" (cf. Lev 19:15,34; Deut 1:16; 16:18; 2 Chron 9:8; Jer 22:3; Zeph 3:5).

To judge, and to bring justice and thereby assistance, is the duty of the king. Hosea 13:10: "Where is your king, that he may help you in all your cities and bring justice?—of whom you said, 'Give me a king and princes!'" (cf. Pss 72:1–14; 7:11–13). But God is Israel's king, and as such he is judge and savior. Psalm 10:16–18: "YHWH is king forever. The Gentiles have perished from the land. You have heard the desire of the afflicted, YHWH, and you have strengthened their heart. You have inclined your ear to bring justice to the orphaned and oppressed. Man, who is of the earth, will terrify no longer." Even Julius Wellhausen and Hermann Schultz recognized that Diestel was wrong to insist that God's kingship in the Old Testament is related infrequently to his theocratic position over Israel and predominantly to his dominion over the world. The opposite is the case. YHWH is Israel's king, and it is Israel's king who triumphs over all the world. Israel is his beloved and chosen people, for whose benefit he exercises his power. God acts in judging righteousness for the redemption of his people, and this action is attributed to his kingship over Israel. "The day of YHWH," "that day" that always constitutes the horizon of the prophetic field of vision, is the day of his kingly display of power in judging righteousness (Isa 24:21–23; 43:14–15; 44:6; Obad 1:15–21; Pss 22:28; 24:7–10; 68:24–31; 74:12–21; 89:18; 93–100; 103:17–19; 145:11–13; 9:4–12).

This kingship of God over Israel rests on free divine election. Connected with this election, this act of the holiness of God, is both the historical redemption from Egypt through his deeds of righteousness (Mic 6:5) as well as the future, promised, and longed-for redemption through the display of his kingly power in the judgment of his righteousness (Pss 33:12; 47:2–4; 78:67–72; 132:13; 135:4; Isa 14:1; 41:8–10; 43:7–10; 44:1–5; 49:7; Jer 33:24; Ezek 20:5; Zech 1:17; 2:12; Ps 105: 6–7,43–44; Isa 65:9,22–23).

Hope in the judging righteousness of God thus points us back once again to the starting point of our knowledge of his attributes, to his holiness displayed in election. The holiness and righteousness of God relate to each other as do calling or election and justification. Righteousness and holiness join together again, and it is by understanding their connection that we can loosen the knot that, according to the common view, seems to be tied precisely here.

This knot is the unavoidable question: How can the holy God, "whose eyes are too pure to look upon evil" (Hab 1:13), intervene in judging righteousness for the right of a people that is not in the right? How should the plea of Psalm 143:1–2 be understood: "Answer me according to your righteousness, and enter not into judgment with your servant, for no one living is righteous before you"? And how is this consistent with the apparently conflicting request of Psalm 7:9, "Judge me, YHWH, according to my righteousness"? The judgment of the righteousness of God is supposed to bring redemption to a sinful people, when they for their part ought to be just as afraid of God's judgment as their oppressors? How is this imaginable? How can a sinner be righteous?

We must ask a further question: What does it even mean to be righteous? What is being righteous? And that not in the sense of Greek ethics, but much more seriously in the sense of the prayer of Psalm 143? Righteousness is everywhere a relational concept, not in the sense of a relation to a highest norm, but in the sense that it describes a relationship between two subjects that involves certain expectations. These expectations, for example, could be for tools, in order to use them rightly; for a journey, so as not to go astray; or for balances and weights, so that they do not deceive (Lev 19:36; Ezek 45:10; Job 31:6; Ps 23:3). They could be expectations that one person places on another. The relationship itself is the norm, and it yields the expectations, the right, that one person has with respect to another. One who is righteous meets the relational expectations placed on him by others, whether God or other people. That is why רָשָׁע is the opposite of צַדִּיק: it involves lies and deceit, it violates the helpless and afflicted, and it treads underfoot the expectations of others. But in Israel God, as king of his chosen people, has the right or the expectations that one has with regard to another who is placed under his protection. The people can exist in no other way. These expectations are the point of the law—not the revelation of moral truth or the formulation of moral tasks and duties. This is why the concept of righteousness acquires at the same time a religious significance. He is righteous who meets the expectations of God and others. He exercises righteousness and is therefore in the right and thus has the righteousness of God for himself.

But it is not only the one who does right who is in the right. He also is in the right, and especially so, who suffers injustice in the hard reality of life. This is how the Old Testament speaks of the righteous. It is they who by their conduct rebuke the injustice of others, and so provoke violence against themselves. They are in the right and therefore suffer injustice. It is now inescapably obvious that those who typically suffer from injustice, the widows and orphans, the poor, the lowly, and the helpless, are described as righteous because they are indeed in the right, and their right stands under the protection of God. Their only hope is the righteousness of God. This is connected to a very significant phenomenon, namely, that even someone who confesses his sins, as did Job (9:2; 14:2), and who must humble himself in the knowledge that "no one living is righteous before you" (Ps 143:2; cf. Ps 130:3), can and may still appeal to the righteousness of God for acknowledgement and protection of his righteous cause (Job 13:18; 16:20–21; 17:8–9; 42:7; Jer 12:1–4).

From this we finally conclude that the one who has received justice through God's intervention, the justified in whose favor God has judged, stands as צַדִּיק. He is righteous who has received justice (Isa 60:21; 45:23–25; 54:17; Zech 9:9–13).

By electing Israel as his people, God becomes the protector of justice within Israel. This is precisely why those who take their religion seriously, and who see it as resting on the fact of this election, have their eyes opened to their own injustice. As soon as the injustice they commit begins to outweigh the injustice they suffer, and the more distinctly they sense God's freedom in electing, and the more prevailing their desire for God's favor to continue, the more unavoidably their appeal to the divine protection of right is bound up with the plea, "enter not into judgment with your servant" (Ps 143:2). Moreover, if they recognize the violence they suffer as the punishment they deserve, where will they find the courage to appeal to the righteousness of God and to the protection of right, the deliverance, that can be expected from it alone?

The significance of the election of Israel, of its singling out and sanctification by the holiness of God, now becomes clear and solves our problem. Ultimately Israel has *not a subjective but only an objective right to redemption*. Israel is a sinful people, and yet it has a righteous cause. Its right before other peoples and against all its enemies is its election. It is a right conferred on Israel, to which Israel must cling. The relationship established by election certainly carries obligations that Israel must fulfill. But this is only so that their election may not be rendered invalid and become rejection.[11] Ul-

---

11. Note that rejection, מאס, does not apply to those who are not elect. It indicates only the annulment of election for the elect: Jer 33:24; Ps 78:59,67–68; Exod 32:32–33;

timately it is not just the conduct demanded by election, but always election itself that establishes the right of Israel. Because of election Israel can and does continue to find forgiveness; through forgiveness, God holds Israel upright. (See especially Isa 43:19–28 as well as the appeal to the faithfulness of God in, e.g., Exod 32:11–14; Deut 9:26–29; Dan 9:15–16; Deut 7:9; 32:4; Isa 49:7; Rom 3:3; 11:29.) It is election alone than enables Israel to carry on. If, because of its sin, Israel is given into the hands of its enemies, and its eyes are thereby opened to its sins, there remains nothing else but to beg for forgiveness. Their own righteousness is thin as a spider's web (Isa 59:5–6), a filthy garment (Isa 64:6); yet the cause for which it is afflicted is a righteous cause. And when it is sufficiently humbled and has received double for its sins, its righteousness will be revealed (Isa 40:1–5; 51:17–23; 54:7–14; 57:14–21; 61; Jer 12:1; Mic 7:9). For though Israel's affliction is punishment from God, its oppressors still commit injustice, for their motive is not to obey the command of God, who appointed them executors of his judgment, but animosity toward the chosen people of God and ultimately toward Israel's God, toward YHWH himself (Isa 49:24–26; 51:22–23). The same righteousness of God that protects the righteous cause of the servant of YHWH (Isa 41:10; cf. 41:2) is also the salvation of the abandoned and once again pardoned people (Isa 54:14–17; 58:8).

It is election alone that enables Israel to trust in God, to hold fast to him, to believe in him, to take refuge in his righteousness in all the affliction and hardship it has endured. In its election, and not in its conduct, Israel has an indisputably righteous cause, against which no one can rise up, for who wants to dispute with YHWH? This righteous cause, election, gives Israel the right to believe and obligates it to believe. The one whom God does not elect does not have this right. Hence, "if you do not believe, neither will you stand" (Isa 28:16; 7:9; Deut 1:30–33; 9:23). To have forsaken him and trusted in other gods and looked to mere flesh for strength (Jer 17:5)—this is the sin for which Israel has always been punished. Consider all the passages in which Israel's sin is identified with the two words לֹא הֶאֱמִין, it did not believe. Again and again Israel must return to the one it has forsaken and confess its sin. There is and can be no other help. The one whom God has not chosen has no hope at all; the one he has chosen has no other help than him.

It now becomes clear that the righteous cause of the people, who were surrendered to their enemies because of their sin, is not moral faultlessness,

---

Isa 14:1; 41:9; Zech 1:17; 2:12. See my *Lexicon*, s.v. ἐκλέγεσθαι.

but holding fast to God, האמין (Gen 15:6; Hab 2:4). This people can take no other action than confessing its sin. Its objective right, one could just as well say, is its religion; its subjective right is its practice of religion, taking its religion seriously. It matters who confesses his sins and seeks again the face of God after the whole people has forsaken God. The prayer for forgiveness is then the only possible expression of holding fast to God. Through election, God has granted them the right to this prayer, and commanded it as a duty. It is at the same time an appeal to the righteousness of God. Election is the objective right of Israel. Repentant faith, as an expression of this objective right, is the subjective right of Israel. And the righteousness of God that hears prayer is at the same time grace for those whom it hears. There is no opposition between righteousness and grace. Rather, the action of righteousness is grace, and the proof of grace is righteousness. Grace is thus also *reward* as recompense for faith. With God's righteousness, there is no difference between grace and reward. The action of judging righteousness is recompense for faith and expectation, yes, even recompense for having suffered injustice (Gen 15:1–6; Isa 40:10; 62:11; Jer 31:16). All is grace and all is reward—except one thing only: the foundation of entitlement to God's righteousness, election.[12]

A magnificent design thus confronts us in the religion of Israel, that is, in what the religion of Israel was intended to be. Only God's righteousness, that is to say, his righteous judgment, can be the refuge of those who suffer injustice. And because injustice fills the whole world, it alone can be the refuge of those who suffer under the constraints of life in this world. However, only someone who has the right to do so may appeal to God's righteous judgment. And nobody has this right except the one whom God has chosen for himself and who, through this election, has come to stand in opposition to the whole world. This one can believe. Only faith has this right. Only to faith is God's judging and saving righteousness revealed. The judging righteousness of God is thus the solution to the riddle of history for those whom God has chosen.

The truth of this design requires no proof, if we have taken the right starting point, namely, that for us as well there is no other connection with God, no other possibility of faith, than that founded upon election. If this is so, then the prospect of God's judging righteousness is for us as well the solution to the riddle of history. It is clearly of the greatest significance that the basic view of the New Testament is the same. This is indicated even

---

12. See my *Lexicon*, s.v. μισθός.

in the proclamation of the kingdom of God and his righteousness for all who have hungered and thirsted for the saving righteousness of God (Matt 6:33; 5:6). This proclamation brings the longed-for forgiveness (Luke 1:77), and the connection of the proclamation of John the Baptist with the rite of baptism shows that the kingdom of God, righteousness, and forgiveness all belong together. "The kingdom of God is at hand" obviously means for Israel that "His righteousness is at hand." The kingship of God, the kingdom of God, the messianic king, the righteousness of God, and the hope of judgment—these all belong inseparably together for Israel. Every tone rings when any one of them is struck. The apostles no longer proclaim the kingdom of God, as did John the Baptist and Christ; they proclaim Jesus Christ, the messianic king. The king takes the place of the kingdom. This is the only difference. Where Christ is named, there the talk is of the kingship and kingdom of God, and the saving righteousness of God along with them. For the chosen witnesses to Jesus are Jews who believe in the Messiah. The hope they have and proclaim is the day of the Parousia. This "oldest dogma in Christendom," belief in the coming day, the last day, and waiting for it as for the day of redemption, marked out from all others the life of faith of the messianic community. It is proof that they, too, just as the Old Testament community of God, waited for and hoped in the judgment of the righteousness of God. What helped them wait was that by faith in Christ they had forgiveness and could therefore hope for it. This is the great contrast with unbelieving Israel and with the records of their hope that have come down to us in the book of 4 Ezra—once this hope had decayed into fear and anxiety. That is also the difference between hope in the New Testament Apocalypse (Rev 6:10; 15:3; 16:5–7; 19:2; cf. 7:14; 16:15; 3:4,18; John 17:25; 1 John 2:29) and what only goes by the name of hope. The one thing that those who believe in Messiah Jesus still lack is the fulfillment of this hope. The electing love of God has turned the Gentiles to itself and in the gospel has offered them faith. This act of God makes faith possible for them. Whoever accepts this act in faith has the righteousness of God for himself. He has forgiveness of sins in the power of the Holy Spirit, the "first fruits" (Rom 8:23) and "guarantee of our inheritance until the redemption of God's possession" (Eph 1:14). He has a righteous cause in and by his faith, in place of his sin. He is righteous and can hope. Upon him God has acted as "just and the one who justifies the wicked by faith" (Rom 3:26; 4:5). He says with all who believe, "Through the Spirit, by faith, we await the hope of righteousness" (Gal 5:5), "for in hope we were saved" (Rom 8:24). These are the elect (Rom 8:28–39), who can take comfort in the future, and who, because of their election and their faith, are called in the New Testament "holy," "holy and beloved," "holy and faithful." They still live in the midst of a world that neither knows God nor believes the gospel. As long as they find themselves in this situation—and it will continue until the gospel of the kingdom is proclaimed to all peoples in the entire world as a testimony to them (Matt 24:14)—so long must they wait upon the righteous judgment of God that makes their right clear and counters that of the world, "since God considers it just to repay with affliction those who afflict you, and to refresh you who are afflicted, with us, in the revelation of Jesus Christ from heaven, coming with the angels of his might in flames of fire, taking vengeance on those who do not know God and do not obey the gospel of our Lord Jesus, and who will suffer the punishment of eternal destruction from the face of the Lord and from the glory of his strength, when he comes to be glorified by his saints and to show himself wonderful to all who have believed" (2 Thess 1:6–10). Once the struggle lies behind them, and they have kept the faith to the end of their course, they can boast with Paul, "before me lies the crown of righteousness that the Lord, the righteous judge, will give to me on that day, and not to me alone, but to all who have longed for his appearing" (2 Tim 4:8).

In this way the one who was called to be an apostle to the Gentiles brought even to the heathen world hope in the righteous judgment of God as the solution to the riddle of history, both collective and individual. He brought what could give them a righteous cause: the gospel of Jesus. This glance at Jesus confirms what we have learned about the judging and saving righteousness of God. No blood on earth, "from the blood of Abel on," has been so unjustly shed as the blood of Jesus. Never has the entire world been so completely unjust as it was—and still is—to Jesus. And everything from his flight to Egypt to his death on the cross he did only for the sake of the cause he was there to accomplish, his calling, for the sake of which he was what he was and wanted to be, the God-given, promised Messiah. Try though one might to find another reason for the sentence of death that fell upon him, there is but one: that he confessed under oath that he was the Christ, the Son of the living God. This is why the world could find no place for him. But he entrusted himself to the one who judges justly (1 Pet 2:23). Now it would be settled whether there is a righteousness of God. It was settled. God intervened for his anointed, but not in such a way that the judgment of posterity would be different from that of Christ's contemporaries.

It is the way of humanity, but not of the righteousness of God, "to build the tombs of the prophets and adorn the graves of the righteous" (Matt 23:29). God judged otherwise, wonderfully in every respect. He did not judge the world that rejected his Christ and their Savior, and yet he did judge justly, for God raised him from the dead and exalted him to his right hand. Jesus has not ceased to be that for which God sent him. He still is this, and so it is still possible—yet another wonder—for the world to come out from its injustice through the only just cause there can be, through faith in Jesus. To bring this about, God appears again in his presence in the Holy Spirit everywhere the word of Jesus is proclaimed, and he will appear on the last day, when the result of his righteous judgment will be the righteous cause of Jesus Christ and of those who believe in him. This is the certainty that is indissolubly bound up with faith and that we cannot escape once we allow God's opposition to our sin have its effect upon us—and it is once again knowledge of this opposition that has formed our starting point.

This is the wonderful righteousness of God that opens itself to us in his revelation. It is the righteousness of the judge, whose essence it is to be justifying and therefore saving righteousness. And its essence is to be this for us sinners and to guarantee for us that we may wait for "a new heaven and a new earth, in which righteousness dwells" (2 Pet 3:13)—a new world that is not the result of human development, but of the judging righteousness of God at the end of days, when this age is superseded by the age to come. There is a judging righteousness of God that is not our terror, but our refuge and hope when we are troubled by the riddle of history, of world history and of our own life. For there is also a righteousness that we sinners can have, the righteousness of faith, that is counted as righteousness and in which we await "the righteousness for which we hope" (Gal 5:5). This is the definition that results: the righteousness of God is the activity of his might in judgment, in accordance with his holiness, in favor of those whom he has chosen, "that they should believe in him for eternal life" (1 Tim 1:16), and who with this faith have a right in the midst of a world that in its wrong is perishing under the law of sin and death that prevails within it. God's holiness and righteousness operate and belong together just as our election and our justification. The rejection of the world that rejected Jesus and resists the Holy Spirit (Acts 7:51)—this simply means that they "do not enter into God's righteousness" (Ps 69:27), that they do not experience justifying righteousness but perish in their sin. The condemnation (κατάκριμα) that befalls them is the opposite of justification (δικαίωσις), and it comes upon them because of their unbelief.

From the attributes of the holiness and righteousness of God we thus learn what appropriate conduct toward him is, which is the essence of revealed religion so long as there is such a thing. It is the one and only true instance of religion, of having God, of actual connection with God, namely, faith, the faith that is counted as righteousness, what the New Testament calls faith in Jesus (πίστις Ἰησοῦ), faith that he is the Christ, faith in "the Lord our righteousness" (Jer 23:6). This result is the test of the validity of what we have learned.

3. THE WISDOM OF GOD

In his revelation, God shows that he alone knows the way out and works out the dark riddle of history. His will for redemption, intended for the sinful world but not to be understood on the basis of the law of consistency, is the only thing that explains why the world still exists. In itself, this world is bound to the law of rational and moral consistency, and so it has no other prospect on its own than to perish under the law of sin and death that dominates it. Only through the equally wonderful execution of God's will in Christ does the world really exist, and only through the execution of this same will, which we experience in ourselves in the working of the Holy Spirit, is the final result of a new world certain for us, a world in which righteousness dwells. There it will be clear, without any obstruction or limitation, what it means and implies to say that God is love, or that, according to his eternal will, he desires to be everything that he is for a world that he created, preserved, and redeemed for this purpose. Thus the knowledge of God's will and of its previous and continuing execution results in the knowledge of the wisdom of God. The wisdom of God is the exaltation of his will for the salvation of the world over the law of consistency, as he has accomplished it, is accomplishing it, and will accomplish it in redemption and its completion. Together with his holiness and righteousness, God's wisdom displays his opposition to sin not in our destruction, as would be reasonable, but "beyond all understanding" (Phil 4:7) in our redemption. One can thus say more precisely that the wisdom of God is the exaltation of his love, which sets goals and arranges the means to achieve them, over the law of consistency, yet without repealing or negating it. This wisdom acts for and upon the sinful world for its redemption, and both brings about and demands our faith. In this connection to the riddle of history and to our redemption, wisdom is important to our religious interests. These are not served by defining wisdom according to its extent and thus quantitatively and generally as infinite wisdom, as is often the custom. Wisdom must rather be recognized as the particular wisdom of the "only wise God" (Rom 16:27).

It is clear that, outside revealed religion, as little can be said about God's wisdom as about his holiness and righteousness. For if the world in its wisdom, outside revealed religion, has not even become aware of the actual riddle of the world, it can hardly know how this riddle can be solved only through God's free will to love and his free act of love. It can therefore come as no surprise that even Greek philosophy—the divine world-reason of Plato's doctrine of the ideas and the Stoic Logos—not only cannot attain knowledge of the wisdom of God, which discloses itself in his revelation, but functions essentially in opposition to it. It also becomes understandable, however, that only where revealed religion comes into contact with the attempt to solve the riddle of existence, and so with the philosophy of the ancient world, would the word "wisdom" be used for the attribute of the one who alone and truly knows how to solve this riddle and does solve it. That is why we first find the concept of the wisdom of God at the time when Israel came into contact with Greek philosophy. The concept is first applied to the world-ordering wisdom of God in general, where it is active not in a transcendent world of ideas, but in the purposeful creation and preservation of the world with its limits and boundaries, and in binding the world to a moral order, to the law (Prov 3:19–20; 8:1–3,22–31; Job 28:24–28). Later, and particularly since God's revelation in Christ crossed over into the territory of the Gentile world, wisdom was applied to the redemptive activity of God as its proper domain. It is "the wisdom, hidden in mystery, which God had decreed beforehand for our glory, which none of the rulers of this world has understood, for if they had understood it, they would not have crucified the Lord of glory" (1 Cor 2:7–8; cf. 1:21). That is why Christ is "the power of God and the wisdom of God" (1 Cor 1:24), and why "all the treasures of wisdom and knowledge are hidden in him" (Col 2:3). Paul praises it as he looks back on the decree of God carried out in election (Rom 11:33), as it will be extolled some day at the end of the ways of God (Rev 5:12; 7:12), and as it appears now and forever glorious to the members of the heavenly realm through the community that is redeemed by it (Eph 3:10). The Scriptures of the old covenant speak of wisdom in relation to redemption when they deal with the will of the one who has no need of a counselor and who carries out his cause gloriously (Isa 29:28; 40:12–28; Pss 25:12; 33:10–11). While we obviously cannot exclude creation and preservation from the domain of wisdom, neither can we be satisfied with the definition that wisdom is the perfection of God's idea of the world, for in this way redemption is brought into necessary connection with creation as the completion of it. The wisdom of God brings it about that, despite the entrance of sin, the purpose of creation does not need to be abandoned. But it becomes clear only from redemption that it was also wisdom that acted to determine the purpose of creation, as indeed it is only from redemption that the purpose and power of the preservation of the world are understood.

So it is not as though there are three realms of equal rank, three co-ordinated expressions—creation, preservation, and redemption—in which God's wisdom is active. Rather, wisdom finds its particular realm and its particular activity in redemption, within which preservation has its purpose and creation regains its purpose. Christian understanding will have to emphasize this increasingly. And the Christian, with his experience of the closed world-system of nature and history, will have to make clear that in this system we are dealing with a life that is independent in itself, and yet that the reign of God that aims at our salvation is so distinct from it that its result is the exact opposite of the world-system. The Christian's faith and hope are not the same as the system of nature in its astounding coherence and power. Although it too is a work of God's hands, its working is not like God's working. Even the phrase "nature *and* God" is no help to the Christian. Just as little is his hope in history and the "reason in history" that derives from Greek philosophy. Any such hope is taken from him by his experience and understanding of the system of history and of the law of sin and death that reigns within it, despite all the activity of the human spirit. The idea of reason in history is for him at best an inadequate attempt to solve the actual riddle of the world. But he can also judge it more soberly and objectively as an attempt to contradict the actual solution to the riddle of the world and confront it with an alternative. But the failure of this idea does help us to recognize and acknowledge the wisdom of God that holds sway over history. It is wisdom that, on the one hand, obliges the persons and the powers who live and lead history, willingly or unwillingly, to serve it and its purposes. On the other hand, wisdom also makes it impossible for them ultimately to thwart God's purposes and goals. Not reason with its might and methods, but God's wisdom alone triumphs, in God's peculiar ways, over sin and death. In Luther's matchless translation, "Since the world in its wisdom did not know God in his wisdom," God has chosen, through the foolishness of proclamation, to save not those who are wise, but those who believe (1 Cor 1:21).

The wisdom of God, which becomes certain for us as his redeeming love works for us and upon us, brings it about and requires that we trust him on dark paths, when the coherence of the world-system and the sense-lessness of history burden those who might have expected things to be otherwise, and who for this reason are directed to hope in the righteousness of God (Ps 73). Here we encounter a riddle that is almost darker than the riddle of history emphasized so far, the riddle of the patience of God, who does not prevent sin and delays sending help to his children. As soon as we recognize that the sinful world has its existence only on the basis of the divine decree of redemption, we also know how it comes about that sin still occurs and still reigns in the world. Even sin itself lives, so to speak, only because God's decree of redemption applies to the world. But despite sin, God's purposes do not come to naught. Indeed, even sin ultimately pertains to God's purpose to bring about redemption (Gen 50:20; Acts 2:23). This too is part of God's exaltation over the law of consistency. The history of the world moves forward under the patience of God. But it is not only patience that God exercises, as we will see in our discussion of the omnipotence of God, but more than patience. It is a particular operation of God's power that he sustains a world that could no longer sustain itself if he were to treat it in a manner strictly consistent with its sin. It would be consistent if he were to unleash upon it his opposition to sin. It is not consistent, but a free act of his love, that he exercises this opposition while sustaining the world for redemption. Thus arises the riddle that the divine preservation of the world entails no less than a reign of sin. To a faith that is certain of the wisdom of God, however, this riddle is solved through consideration of the quiet ways of God in election, from the election of Israel to the era of world missions in which we live. For world mission is nothing other than the execution of divine election upon and within the Gentile world. This perception, the experience of divine election through the call of the word of the gospel of Christ and through the working of his Holy Spirit, shows us the ways God's wisdom chooses and thus sustains in us the confidence that he will most certainly lead his purposes to their goal. The entire world-system, in which we see more and more a deliberately uniform human life, must serve this mission and thereby the electing will of God. For the promised end will not come before the gospel of the kingdom of God is proclaimed in all the world to all peoples as a testimony to them (Matt 24:14). This is the certainty that faith in God's wisdom gives us, and this is also the understanding of history that arises from knowledge of God's wisdom. The entire historical life of humanity, both in the display of the abundance of its powers as well as in the experience of its limitation by the law of sin and death, must serve to make humanity ready and willing to receive redemption, the self-offering of God in electing love. What appears as a delay in the fulfillment of the promise is actually God's patience, which he exercise in his wisdom, so that everything that happens, whether for good or evil, may serve one purpose and goal: to save those who want to be saved.

God's exaltation over the law of consistency does not exclude the closed system of his ways. This system cannot be any more unified and closed than it is. But neither does it negate this law, but rather confirms it, since God impels us to an unqualified acknowledgment of it precisely in his revelation. But there can be absolutely no limitation of God through the law of consistency. God conducts himself consistently toward us when he allows us to experience, and compels us to recognize, the problem between our sin and his opposition to it. But in his revelation God conducts himself beyond all consistency as our redeemer, when he offers us the opposite of what would be consistent for us. For it is obvious that the revelation of redemption is not the consistent result of our conduct. Faith cannot bear to call redemption the consistent execution of the divine purpose for the world. At the very least this would suggest that God's purpose for the world requires him to redeem the world once it has become sinful. To admit any kind of consistency between redemption and God's purpose for the world or for himself is impossible for a faith whose stability is the absolute freedom of the divine election. The faith that God has brought about knows that the one who has begun a good work desires to complete it, and will do so (Phil 1:6). Indeed, that he will do so in such a way that emphasizes again at every point both the opposition to consistency in relation to us and to our sin as well as the unconditional faithfulness of love—a love that proceeds not according to the law of development, but according to the contrary rule: where sin increased, grace abounded all the more (Rom 5:20). That is why the consistent conclusion to God's ways and goals, as known from revelation, is something other and still more certain than the conclusion of reason concerning what is consistent.

By knowing the wisdom of God in his revelation, the Christian acquires a sure teleology of the world-system. It is not as though the world is supposed to serve something lying beyond it, nor as though Christian scholarship were now required to discover a particular final purpose for every individual phenomenon in order to understand the whole. Every particular thing will be understood within the system of cause and effect in which it appears, and indeed according to the law that everything is seed and everything is fruit. If we could perceive God and recognize the power that flows from him, from his revelation, and obligates and entitles us to faith, then we could also recognize, in light of his revelation, those workings of God in which his counteraction of sin appears, both in his judgments in history and in the ways of his election. It is then the duty of the Christian community, when the opportunity presents itself, to investigate and ponder these clues. That is the part of history that it must understand. At the same time it must not be blind to the closed system of history of the world's life in itself, which God's revelation is determined to counteract and against which the world is directed to trust God's wisdom and to hope in the final judgment of his saving righteousness. As we recognize *ourselves* as the final purpose of the divine self-revelation, we recognize ourselves and our salvation also as the final purpose of all being and occurrence. For in our salvation, God counteracts our sin and he also exercises that patience that has allowed the reality of the reign of sin to exist, thus obliging us to wait upon the still-future revelation of his righteousness. Everything that exists and happens does so for us. It is we who are the fruit and the effect of everything that happens, even of things that happened thousands of years ago. We should relish the victories both of the Greeks over the Persians and of the Romans over the Carthaginians as well as the election of Abraham and the redemption of Israel from Egypt. Everything past and present presses together ever more urgently upon the generation that experiences the final escalation of the opposition between God and history, between the final outcome of history and the goal and end of the ways of God who opposes this final outcome. This is the certainty of faith in the wisdom of God who actively opposes sin in holiness and righteousness, the certainty of faith in the perfect execution of his will to solve the riddle of history through redemption.

Holiness, righteousness, and wisdom are the three attributes of God in which his opposition to sin comes to expression as it shapes his revelation.

While other attributes are typically listed among those that are disclosed in revelation, they are not distinct attributes, but only modes in which these three appear. God's inviolability and purity, for example, are included in his holiness. His goodness, mercy, grace, faithfulness, and truthfulness are expressions of his righteousness. His forbearance and patience belong to his wisdom. God's working toward our redemption in holiness, righteousness, and wisdom is not the consistent outcome of his dominion over the world and his opposition to sin. It is the act of his love, absolutely free, whose essence is to be exalted over the law of deductive and moral consistency. The truth of the knowledge of God in revealed religion demands and produces faith. It cannot be the result of a supposed intellectual-moral development, whether of a privileged people or of an above-average degree of character, nor an achievement or discovery of the spirit that thrives in its knowledge of the world-system. The religions are products of the human spirit, as is the attempt to improve them by transposing them into philosophy. But the religion that truly is religion, that truly is connection with God—indeed, the connection of sinners with God—rests entirely and exclusively on revelation, on God's self-manifestation in love that transcends all consistency. Through this love, we recognize and experience that the relationship between God and the world does not take place under the power of eternal, immutable laws, but in freedom. This freedom alone gives us a living God. It would be the death of God if he and the ways he relates to the world were bound to the law of consistency. There would then be no need of God. He would be basically nothing other than the law of consistency already in force in the world, the connection between cause and effect, which would destroy all personal life and every personal relationship. There would be no place for freedom or moral standards. Constraint is the opposite of power, and power is freedom. Only the free power of God raises us above the closed world-system to freedom in the faith that God's truth demands and produces. In his power and freedom God is the living God, who alone and truly is God. Because he freely does as he pleases with himself, in order to be for us everything that he is, we have life by him and in him, eternal life, for the living God is not the God of the dead, but of the living (Matt 22:32).

This is how we know that the God of revelation, the Holy One of Israel, the God of our fathers, the Father of our Lord Jesus Christ alone and truly is God. This is also how we know what it actually means for him to be God, or what the whole entire content of the predicate "God" is. This also indicates how we should understand the concept of an attribute that is implicit in the predicate "God." The God who acts in freedom to be for us everything that he is—he is, as Lord of himself, also Lord of those notions that are gathered up in the predicate "God" and that describe his relation to the world. The predicate "God" means that the one to whom it belongs is the power absolutely superior to the world. It is also the term for a unique relationship that binds the world but not God. God is free in his relation to the world; the world is bound to him. The binding of the world to God, in the various relations that are posited in the distinction between contingent and absolute being, yields the divine attributes of omnipotence, omnipresence, omniscience, eternity, and immutability. Our task is now to understand these attributes as attributes of the God of revelation, so that we may also see their significance for the purpose of God, for our redemption, and so for our faith.

We must therefore note from the outset a twofold result of what we have learned thus far. First, the affirmation that the Father of our Lord Jesus Christ, the God of revelation, alone and truly is God—this is an affirmation of faith. But so likewise are the attributes noted above that constitute the concept of God. They are affirmations of faith. They can be explained on the basis of no other reality than the object of faith. Only faith can see in the heavens, for example, witnesses to the power of God. And second, none of these attributes operates with any kind of natural necessity, even if it goes by the title of a necessity of the divine essence. They do not function immediately and automatically any time they come into contact with another being. God's attributes are his will. The attributes are not lord over God; God is Lord of his attributes. They all serve him and must do so if they are to act toward us in freedom and bring about our freedom. If in unexpected and marvelous freedom God still displays his opposition to our sin, which we at the mere thought of God already feel as opposition, how much less will the attributes posited in the concept of God be active apart from his will. Initially they are only formal determinations; their content they receive from their subject.

4

Second Series

Divine Attributes Implicit in the Concept of
God, Seen in Light of Revelation

1. THE OMNIPOTENCE OF GOD

From the reality of redemption faith learns both the reality of divine omnipotence as well as the content of this concept. In his revelation, God displays his opposition to the sinful world in so wonderful a way as to redound to its redemption. God has forever bound both the world and its fate to himself, and only to himself. Whoever recognizes in Christ, whom God has given to us, the fact of his own redemption and liberation from the otherwise crushing uniformity of the world-system—such a person sees this as the free act of one who is more powerful than the entire world. God acts in the self-realization of his love in absolute freedom. He is not bound by the law of consistency that makes the world-system inescapable for others. For the one for whom this God acts, nothing is impossible. This is God's omnipotence. It is the opposite of what can be known from either experience or investigation of the world-system in nature and history. Only the Christian, only the one who knows God from his revelation, knows that God is omnipotent. For only the Christian has the proof of this in his faith, which revelation both requires of him and produces in him. It is a peculiar and significant phenomenon that nowhere do we encounter so deep a feeling for the vast, tightly-closed, systematic interconnectedness of life in this world—and this despite our inadequate knowledge of nature—as in the sphere of revealed religion. And it is precisely here, among the devout, the servants of God of the Old and New Testaments, that we find the most resolute faith in the omnipotence of God. The idea of the omnipotence of God does not contradict the reality of this system. It is actually through God's relationship to this system that this idea receives its full wealth and power. *The omnipotence of God is the superior strength of the God of redemption over the self-contained world-system in nature and history.* It is the transcendence of the power of his love over the law of the world-system and active within it. It is the determination of his power through love, in which he desires to be for us everything that he is. His power has no limits other than the will of his love or other than himself. The world is thus totally bound to him and to him alone—even and precisely that world that wants to live from and through itself and to know nothing about God.

It is thus obvious to a Christian that everything apart from God, the entire world, owes its existence and continuation to the omnipotence of God. Redemption is for the Christian the proof of the creation and preservation of the world by God. For just this reason the Christian knows that God's omnipotence is not exhausted in creation and preservation. It is certainly not exhausted in creation, for preservation is already an act of greater power, and redemption and its application to the world are acts of still greater power. Like redemption, creation too is a free act of his love, for there is nothing that could have compelled him to do it. We have already spoken of God's freedom in creation and of how we become aware of it. Still more is preservation a free act of God's almighty love. In consistency, this world can only perish in itself under the law of sin and death that reigns within it. The continued existence of such a world is only possible through an exceptional act of God's power in connection with his intention to redeem. Only on the basis of God's decision to redeem may we sing, "What our God created has, that will he preserve," or confess that he "sustains all things by the word of his power" (Heb 1:3). Omnipotence proves and demonstrates itself further in all of God's acts to execute and implement his determination to save, from the redemption of Israel from Egypt to the resurrection of Christ to the final execution of his righteous judgment in the consummation of salvation. Without redemption, the fact of the existence of a world actively opposing the will of God would be an insoluble riddle and the most weighty evidence against the omnipotence of God. But the revelation of salvation solves this riddle and allows us to recognize that

God does indeed have power over the world, a most wonderful power, in the fact that he preserves such a world for redemption. Thus the Christian knows that the world-system is not almighty, but that this system is only effective through the power of God, and is at the same time limited by it. But it is the redemption of the sinful world that is the highest act of the love that is both omnipotent and free in its omnipotence. The judgment of damnation against the world is the powerful self-assertion of the divine independence and freedom over against a creature that continues and asserts its godless self-life even against redemption.

It is hardly necessary to recall the verses of Scripture that speak either of God's omnipotence, which according to Mark 10:27 can alone bring about our blessedness and salvation, or of faith's confidence in this power, as Paul expresses it in Romans 8:31–39. But this becomes especially important when we recognize that our faith is ascribed to the power of God, indeed, to the same power that raised and exalted Christ (Eph 1:19–21; cf. 1 Pet 1:5; 1 Tim 6:15; 1 Cor 2:5; 2 Cor 6:7; 12:9; Eph 3:7,20; 2 Tim 1:8). The hope of Israel is based on God's power, which puts Israel in the position to carry out his will (Pss 33:8–12; 115:2–13; 135:4–14; Isa 50:2; 59:1). Power appears particularly where God is at work in connection with the revelation of salvation, even when this takes the form of punishment (Jer 32:17–27; Isa 14:27). The effectiveness of those who serve his saving will comes from his power (Acts 6:8; 1 Thess 1:5; 1 Cor 2:5; Col 1:29), for God himself is with them in the Holy Spirit (Luke 24:49; Acts 1:8; 10:38; Rom 15:13–19; 2 Tim 1:7; 1 Pet 4:14). The Spirit and power belong together, for in the Spirit, the innermost being of God, God is present in his power for us and over us, so that "the Spirit of God" and "the power of God" are synonymous. This is why the gospel is the power of God to save those who believe it (Rom 1:16; 1 Cor 1:18,28). The kingdom of God comes in power (Mark 1:7–8; 1 Cor. 4:19–20). Where God is praised as the God of salvation, whether for a present act of salvation or for the completion of his entire counsel and will for the redemption of his people, there his power is also praised and finds its place in all doxologies (Matt 6:13; Eph 3:20–21; 1 Tim 6:16; Rev 7:12; 11:17; 12:10; 15:8; 19:1). Following the custom of the Rabbis, Jesus even uses "Power" as God's name (Matt 26:64; cf. Heb 1:3). That God is designated "the only Sovereign" (1 Tim 6:15) follows naturally where the gospel of the kingdom of God in his truth is recognized and believed. For even the proclamation of the Christ, the messianic King, is indeed the proclamation of the kingship and kingdom of God, and where his kingship is proclaimed, there will his power also be attested, along with his saving righteousness.

If this explanation of God's omnipotence is correct, particularly concerning the origin and verification of our knowledge of it in saving revelation, then it is impossible to accept any limitation of God, even self-limitation, with respect to the creature. The omnipotence of God would not be something that is active in freedom, but would produce its effects with irresistible necessity in the manner of a law of nature, if it were a sole causality and so excluded any effectiveness of creaturely causality. Creaturely causality, the so-called "secondary causes," has the capacity to produce effects, but this causality is itself produced by the power of God. Its effectiveness is his will, and since there is no arbitrariness of will with him, there can hardly be limitation of his power in the existence and effectiveness of these secondary causes, since in them it is indeed only his will that comes to expression. Of course, this is also why God's power rules out any arbitrary outburst of their effectiveness—especially an arbitrary outburst. We must also insist that God is not bound to his particular purposes, once these purposes require something else. This follows from his transcendence over the law of contingent being. God has placed on contingent being definite limits, which are inseparable from contingency, in such a way that these limits actually enable the full exertion of the power that it has and in which it acts, and every transgression of these limits must destroy this power and its wielders themselves. God is also capable of working against creaturely effectiveness, and so against the system of nature with its laws, yet without abolishing it, where its result would conflict with his will to redeem. God is just as capable, on the other hand, of serving this effectiveness in freedom and directing it, in connection with his will to redeem, toward his purposes. This why miracles are possible. Miracles cannot be justified more erroneously than by appeal to God's power to do simply anything. As the Almighty, God must be able and is able to work just as well through creaturely, secondary causes as without them, and elicit simply through his word and command what is usually the result of the system of nature. The reply to such an appeal is that God, as his revelation directly proves, never works in contradiction to himself, nor can he do so. This would be the case if he desired to do that which, according to his will, lies in the sphere of creaturely effectiveness, yet without this effectiveness and surpassing it. The essence of miracles lies not in surpassing of the system of nature, but in counteracting it. This counteraction is tied to the will of God, which is both unified in itself and effective for the world, and which, for the sinful world, turns out to be a will to redeem. Such counteraction would not be necessary if there were no sin. Because of sin, the closed system of creaturely being would only end up in destruction, were it not that God's transcendence over the law of this system allows him this wonderful counteraction. God's will to redeem does not abolish his will to create, and yet it establishes a purpose that is opposed to the outcome of what is natural. This makes it clear that God does not abolish the system of nature when he counteracts it in individual instances as required by redemption. The day on which he makes an end of the whole system that now exists, and to which the working of all miracles prophetically points, is the day on which he "makes all things new" (Rev 21:5), a new heaven and a new earth, in which righteousness dwells, "so that the former things will not be remembered nor come to mind" (Isa 65:17). Miracles are the powerful acts of the God of redemption. They would not take place without his particular action. Nor do they take place when he uses creaturely powers, effective within the world-system, to bring about what they would not achieve without his will. For the Christian, this closes the way of escape by double-entry bookkeeping, according to which the operations of nature in general are to be regarded from a religious perspective as operations of God, for in this case they should all be considered miracles.

If God is in any way limited by creaturely causality, even at the level of the system of nature, how much more must he be limited, and to that degree impotent, when it comes to his relation to free creatures, to humans. The claim that God is by no means omnipotent over human freedom, is absolutely false. It is in fact precisely with respect to human freedom that God is and shows himself to be omnipotent. The question of divine omnipotence would otherwise have no meaning. Rather, it is the very omnipotence of God that makes human freedom even possible. Only if God were not almighty, but bound, that is, restricted in his power—only then could he not tolerate creaturely freedom. But now we know through the revelation of redemption that the operation of God's omnipotence brings about not the sheer extermination of human freedom, albeit only eventual, but the restoration of the human freedom that was lost. Through the offer of salvation in electing love, God enables humanity to act for the first time in freedom, in the act of faith, when otherwise, without this election, it would remain forever subject to the bound will (*servum arbitrium*). But in the faith that is based on and produced by God's effective accomplishment of his will to redeem, a person is set free from the destructive law of sin and death that enslaves both him and the entire world. In the midst of the world-system that still oppresses him, he awaits the "glorious freedom of the children of God" (Rom 8:21), in which their life, now unhindered and uninhibited, will display everything now locked up within it. The fact of sin is no exception to the boundlessness of the divine omnipotence. God tolerates sin but need not do so. He allows it to happen. He even preserves by his omnipotence the world in which it reigns. He does not suppress it by force, but bears up the world, yet only because he can and will exercise the omnipotence of his love for its redemption. The fact of God's patience with sin should not cause the Christian to reach for an explanation in terms of divine self-limitation. The opposite is required: a vigorous exercise of faith in the divine omnipotence, which alone is able not merely to endure such a world, but even to uphold it. To recognize and acknowledge God's omnipotence is entirely a matter of faith and is only possible for faith in the revelation of redemption. The compatibility of creaturely freedom with divine omnipotence cannot be demonstrated more clearly than through the revelation of redemption in its significance for restoring and claiming our freedom. But where this almighty love of God is rejected, instead of the restoration of freedom there comes its final destruction. For damnation is the destruction of freedom, whose place is taken by the impotent and trembling belief of the demons in "weeping and gnashing of teeth."

The freedom with which God endowed humanity thus glorifies the divine omnipotence. Even our misuse of freedom, its exercise against God's will, must also serve to call forth a demonstration of the omnipotence and freedom of God, in which the entire fullness of freedom is revealed.

All of the mistakes made in discussions of God's omnipotence come from beginning elsewhere than with the reality of omnipotence, as it gives itself to be known and experienced by us in God's self-manifestation in revelation. Theologians try to acquire this knowledge instead by deductive reasoning. So they define omnipotence as the unity of the divine will and ability, or conclude from this definition that every divine work is necessary, including both creation and redemption. Apart from the fact that correspondence between the divine will and ability is not the same thing as their unity, it is completely inappropriate to apply the concept of necessity to God. It contradicts the actual transcendence of God over anything that could be called a law. The concept of necessity is only valid where there is law. But law only exists in the sphere of contingent, created being. For God there exists only freedom. Creaturely freedom is distinguished from divine freedom in that, within the creaturely sphere, freedom and dependence are and remain intertwined. This is also why we are incapable of solving the antinomy between freedom and necessity except by bearing in mind the reasons that forbid the application of the concept of necessity to God.

2. THE OMNIPRESENCE OF GOD

Created being is contingent being; contingent being is finite being. For created being, restriction in space and time is the form of finitude. At the same time, the creature's restriction to the form of its existence does not imply God's restriction in his relation to the creature, just as the fact of the creature's existence does not imply any limitation of God's power and freedom. Neither the existence nor the particularity of the creature forms any sort of limit on God. God's transcendence over contingent being is, it must be said, also a transcendence over the law of contingent being in every respect. Yet this does not abolish or negate this law and contingent being along with it. This is why God's transcendence of this law is a transcendence of space and time, which does not impede this law, but makes possible the things of which he is capable, not merely to put himself in relation to us, but to remain so, so that we also, beyond space and time, can have him who wants to be for us and with us everything that he is. God restricts created being to the form of existence of space, but God is not restricted in his action in and upon the world. This is what we usually designate as his omnipresence, but which we might more properly, equally extensively, and less abstractly call his world-presence.

It is not through such considerations, however, that our knowledge of the omnipresence of God arose. The idea itself is inseparable from religion and has its origin in it. All religion, even irreligion and heathenism, in so far as it involves a search for God and so reckons with the concept of God, connects the idea of the otherworldliness of the divinity with the idea of at least a certain transcendence of the limitations of space. Philosophy tries to conceive of an actual world-presence of God by way of pantheistic speculation concerning the problem of the independence of God in distinction from the world and in comparison with it. But only the religion of revelation knows and can know God's world-presence if the relation between God and the world is in fact as we experience it to be in revelation, that is, a relation in which we are entirely dependent on the freely demonstrated love of God. Outside of revealed religion, people look for God, but do not know that he "is not far" from each one of us (Acts 17:27). Revelation, however, the action of God for our redemption, tells us that he "is near." Through revelation alone—not through instructive explanations and notifications of findings—but through the particular, this-worldly conduct of the love of the other-worldly God there arises the knowledge of his actual world-presence as a certainty of faith, to which we recognize ourselves obligated and which God brings about in us. It thus arises by way of religion. Indeed, like religion itself, real religion, real connection with God, it arises through divine initiative. The specifically Christian knowledge of God's world-presence, which is distinct from Israel's knowledge of it as fulfillment is to promise, arises and is built up by faith in Christ and by the experience of the presence of God in Christ and in preaching about Christ. We know and experience it through the activity of the Holy Spirit upon us. This knowledge, like the presence of God, is not the possession of individuals, but of the community, which is "a dwelling place of God in the Spirit" (Eph 2:22). As such, it gratefully sings, "God is present, let us adore him!" (Tersteegen). And it awaits the time when the glory of the Lord will fill the world "as the waters cover the sea" (Hab 2:14). The presence of God, by whose power the congregation is what it is, is the practical proof that the limitations of space do not separate God from the world, nor the world from God. Although he is not present to the world everywhere in the same way, he is present to it everywhere and becomes present to it along the way of world missions just as he does to the congregation. The Christian knows that he has been sought and found, and that his congregation has been made into one body, through the calling, gathering, illuminating, and sanctifying word, in the power of the Holy Spirit, who has enabled him to possess God in faith. He thus knows a world-presence of God that no one can know anything about except through this activity of God in connection to his revelation, through which we first discover what kind of God the world has.

We are thus directed once again, as in all of our previous discussions, to the same reality, perceived in faith, as the basis for our statements concerning the world-presence of God. It is impossible by way of conceptual consistency, by means of comparison and contrast between God's transcendence and our restriction to space, between our finitude and his infinitude, or even between spirit and matter, to obtain knowledge of the fact and manner of God's world-presence. If it were possible to build up such a framework, it would then be necessary merely to insert into it the concept of love, as the expression of the essence of God, in order to fill this form with Christian content. But God's omnipresence is not a matter of his way of existing in distinction from the world but, as with all of the attributes, of how God relates himself effectively to the world. For knowledge of God's world-presence, we are thus directed to the reality of God's free activity. The fact of the freedom of God in his activity makes futile from the outset any attempt to acquire knowledge of the fact and manner of this activity apart from its reality.

If we begin from the fact of the world-presence of God that secures the Christian, then we know this fact not as mere presence in the world from beyond, as if God and the world were merely adjacent but non-overlapping. We know it as a presence in the world. Yet this is not in the way that everything which, by its appearances and powers, belongs to the world-system is coordinate with it and therefore bound to it and thus to place. God's world-presence is superordinate over the world-system and acts in this superordination upon everything in the world. The world is not the place of God to which he is bound. So there is no place for him in the world in the way that there is for everything that belongs to the world. Wherever something is, wherever something occurs, there too is God. But he is not there as the power operative in the world and perceptible in all its appearances as an aspect of its continued existence, like some world soul that is inseparable from the world. For God conducts himself in freedom toward everything that is and occurs. God's general world-presence teaches us the same lesson we learned regarding the preservation of the world through the omnipotence of God. God's world-presence is not a necessary implication of the difference between God's mode of being, as the one who is determined by nothing and himself determines all things, and the world's mode of being. Rather, it rests on the free exertion of his powerful will, through which he preserves everything that is and relates himself to everything that is and occurs. The way God exerts himself for the world and relates himself to the world are not necessary for God but for the world and everything in it. The divine world-presence thus finds in God its possibility, in the freedom of his love its actuality, and in the contingency of the world its necessity.

But God relates himself not just to the whole world, so that the individual is only sustained through the whole and is only mediately the object of God's upholding and preserving power. God relates to the whole and to the part, for the whole, like the part, exists for those to whom God desires to be and is what he is. The separation of the whole and the part is an abstraction whose inadmissibility quickly becomes clear, as soon as one puts the question concretely and considers what at first appears to speak against God's self-relation to the individual, namely, sin. Is God also there, where sin occurs? To deny this would mean that sin could and does only happen where God is not present and because he is not present. But sin does not happen because God withdraws his presence, but because people do not pay attention to God and his presence. Although God hands people over to sin as punishment, those whose eyes are open to their punishment will recognize this handing over to the power of sin as a sign of and witness to the effective presence of God, from whose hand the sinner cannot escape, even if God "removes his hand." God no longer upholds him, he abandons him, but he does not expel him from his presence and thus from his judgment. God's presence does not work the same everywhere, but it works everywhere, even in the misery of God-forsakenness. God does not commit sin, but he is where it occurs. That is the wonderful thing about the presence of God, and it is to be understood in the same way as his preservation of the sinful world, from which he does not withdraw in his will to love, but remains present with it, most wonderfully in the world's sin against Christ. But if the presence of God cannot be barred even by sin, then there is still far less reason to deny his presence to the individual within the world-system and to relate it only to the whole. Not even a sparrow falls from the roof without the Father in heaven. Where anything is and occurs, there is God. And yet it is not the case that everything that exists and occurs does so through him. Only faith knows and understands this presence of God, and yet faith knows still more than this general world-presence of God.[1]

That presence of God, on the basis of which faith is certain of his general world-presence, is his saving presence in his particular work of redemption. Where God acts in electing love and thus establishes a particular connection between himself and humanity, there is his saving presence. We experience God's saving presence in the saving activity of the Holy Spirit in word and sacrament. Whoever has become aware of the power of the revelation of God that demands and produces faith knows of a particular

---

1. It may not be necessary to review what Holy Scripture says of God's world-presence, as in Ps 139; Jer 23:23; Acts 17:27; Matt 10:29. Likewise the statements concerning the nearness of God to those who call to him, as in Ps 145:18, etc. In order not to be overly detailed in what follows, and not to over-extend myself in writing, I refer to my *Lexicon*, s.v. πνεῦμα, οὐρανός, ἀποκαλύπτειν; as well as to my article "Geist, heiliger" in the *Protestantische Real-Encyklopädie*, 3rd ed. (Leipzig, 1899) 6:444–50.

dealing of God with us, one that proceeds "according to election" in the world and within its historical life. In this action of God in the Holy Spirit, or in his saving presence, God reveals to those upon whom he acts his innermost being (1 Cor 2:11), and with it everything else God's presence in the world includes within itself. To express it imaginatively, God's saving presence is the center of his presence in the world. Standing within it, one sees that God's world-presence is no operation from beyond or from afar. For God's saving presence is his dealing with us person to person. Indeed, it is a dealing that is ordered toward the most perfect fellowship, toward a fellowship in love that goes far beyond all human fellowship in love. For in it we must and can possess God entirely, and so possess him as no human can possess another. This fellowship becomes a life of God within us and, on our side, a life in God (not merely through him), in which he causes his Spirit to work in us as a new natural power of our life. God, as the God of our salvation, thus becomes connected with those on and in whom he demonstrates his electing love. And thus arises the community of God, the community of salvation, joined together through this act that both elects and frees it from the community of the world. The community of salvation is the place of the saving presence of God that is intended for the entire world. From this place, through witness and the loving service of the community, God's saving presence must be made known to the entire world, and it desires to be made known to it and to act upon it. This is the significance of missionary communities and missionary work. Escorted by missionaries, God's saving presence confirms the testimony of his messengers. God attests himself as present and effective in his saving presence to those who do not know him and upon whom he has never before acted in this way. He can be known and received by them in the power of his revelation that demands and produces faith, so that they too become aware of the fact of the particular, effective presence of God. This is the basis for that receiving of the word that testifies to salvation and to the hour of the visitation of God's grace, which Paul experienced: "When you received from us what God gave to be heard, you received it not as the word of man, but according to what it really is, the word of God, which shows itself effective also in you who believe" (1 Thess 2:13).

It now also becomes clear how there can be a knowledge or certainty of this presence of God even when it is perceived as an inescapable omnipresence, and before it has been recognized as saving presence and become the cause and object of trusting faith. For our perception of the obligating power of all of God's revelatory activity is always the first effect of his opposition to our sin as it makes itself known. This opposition awakens our conscience to self-conviction of both our sin and our liability to judgment. We may not immediately perceive and understand in this our right to trusting faith, but psychologically the reason is easy to see. Faith, as noted above, cannot continue except by vigorous execution of judgment upon itself, from which we must be rescued by the salvation of God. It is this compulsion to self-judgment that causes vacillation between accepting and rejecting the gospel. When a gospel-attesting congregation has to instruct the members born into its fellowship in order to bring them up in the faith and in the community of salvation, as in historic Christianity, it is almost inevitable that for long periods and almost regularly it is only the guilty conscience that individuals are certain of, despite their belonging to the community of the presence of God. This is even the case where instruction in the faith has a clear awareness of its task, but also where neither those called to instruct nor the congregation itself live in faith. The latter scenario is but testimony to the obligating power of truth still inherent even in the remnants of Christendom. This power's gladdening and freeing content must of course remain hidden until the arrival of those who know "something whole about the gospel."

This also shows us the problem with the claim that God's presence is the more perfect, the greater the creature's capacity for it. It is not the presence of God that varies, but the ways in which God works in his presence. And God's working, again, is not determined merely by the need or behavior of its object. Rather, in view of its manifestation to the Gentiles, it must be seen in connection both with God's execution of his will for missions through the community, as well as with the time and hour of his self-manifestation that he himself has chosen in his freedom and wisdom.

If we now return to the distinction between God's saving presence and his general world-presence, we see that this saving presence at work in the congregation, or this presence whose place is the congregation, finds objective expression in word and sacrament as the means of the appropriation of salvation. God's presence in the congregation does not do away with the distinction between God and the congregation, nor is it transformed into the divinity of the congregation, not even at the completion of salvation. For the fellowship between God and the congregation is even in its uniqueness a fellowship in love. It is thus entirely legitimate to speak of the presence of God in word and sacrament. God's presence is the content of word and sacrament: the word attested as living, the sacrament considered in its use. It would conflict with the concept and the essence of the presence of God, which is strictly an efficacious and active presence, to speak of a divine presence available in the means of grace even apart from their use, as for example in the monstrance according to Roman doctrine. The presence of God in word and sacrament even apart from their presentation and their use would mean a trapped, bound presence, the opposite of the actual presence of God.

Because the saving presence of God is only the result of his revelation in Christ, and the witness to his saving presence only occurs through the witness of the gospel to Christ, it is clear that the power that demands and produces faith proceeds from Christ. Faith is faith in Christ. Faith knows in Christ a unique presence of God that is different than his presence in the congregation. Christ is, like the Father, the object of faith.[2] Christ does not have the Father in the same way that the congregation should have him. Rather, the Father's presence in Christ is like the presence in word and sacrament, one that shows itself in its effect on us or on the congregation. It has an effect *on* the congregation, and so is different from both congregation and its own working, just as its presence in word and sacrament. Certainly Christ belongs to us, to the congregation, but he is not coordinate with it as one of its members. Because he belongs to us as no human can belong to another, he is superordinate over us, just as God the Father of our Lord Jesus Christ in his saving presence is not coordinate with the congregation but superordinate over it. Word and sacrament only have their effect because they make us present and effective with the Father and Christ, because God in Christ works through them. So there is a particular presence of God in Christ, and because this presence is a presence of God in his Holy Spirit, God's saving presence is actually the presence of the Triune God.

This yields a twofold conclusion, both backwards and forwards. Backwards, because now every electing act of God, which has as its purpose the sending of Christ, stands out from God's general world-presence as a revelation-presence, without yet being his saving presence in Christ.[3] Where God deals with Israel, there he is present. Indeed, every act of God

---

2. See my *Lexicon*, s.v. πίστις, πιστεύω; as well as my *Prinzipienlehre*, §§4–5, in Zöckler, ed., *Handbuch der theologischen Wissenschaften*, 3rd ed. (Munich, 1890) 3:62–76.

3. Compare God's dwelling with Israel in his sanctuary with the sanctuary's relation to the messianic future, and the prayer of Solomon in 1 Kings 8 with the words of Jesus in John 4:22,24 (cf. John 7:39; Deut 10:14; Isa 66:1; Matt 5:34–35).

takes place in accordance with his saving purpose through his Spirit, his innermost being. That is why every manifestation of God, every revelation, every display of power to Israel is ascribed to his Spirit. And each of these is an act of God for the fulfillment of the promise. Then in Christ he first becomes present to Israel as he had not yet been up until that point. Even Israel's treatment of Christ belongs to God's saving purpose. For God intended, against the sin that was active in total opposition to him, to display his redeeming love: Nevertheless and Notwithstanding. This makes it clear that the saving presence of God we now enjoy is only the result of the history that took place at that time.

Forwards, we face the prospect that, at the end of the ways of God in the world, the ways of mission, we will know a presence of God in which there is no longer a distinction between his general world-presence as based on his will to save and his presence in his community (1 Cor 15:28; Rev 21:2–3). The distinction then will be between this presence and his judging presence to the lost.

From these distinctions in the worldly presence of the otherworldly God, yet another distinction becomes clear. This distinction is between the way in which the presence of God is experienced in the world, and how it is experienced by those who leave this earthly world-system and then experience the completion of either their distance from God or their nearness to him. Because God's this-worldly presence does not nullify his otherworldliness, we will one day appear before him, and our belonging to this earthly world-system will no longer determine the way in which we perceive God. And this experience of God is determined both by God's conduct toward us in his world-presence and by our conduct toward him.

But because God's this-worldly presence does not nullify his otherworldliness, we are both entitled and obligated to distinguish God's current, this-worldly presence from his otherworldliness and thus from his existence beyond this world, i.e., his existence in heaven. Yet this does not mean that we should think of a heavenly place of God in a this-worldly, spatial sense. His this-worldly presence is at the same time a presence from out of his otherworldliness, from heaven, from which he will also reveal himself on the day of the completion of salvation, for the purpose of the display of his judging righteousness. As the idea of God's other-*worldliness* has already indicated, we cannot express this otherwise than in the form of a spatial relationship. And yet, as likewise implied in the idea of *other*-worldliness, this spatiality cannot be meant in a this-worldly sense. The "right hand of God" to which Christ has been exalted is everywhere and still otherworldly. Indeed, it is everywhere precisely because it is otherworldly. At one and the same time, it is this-worldly and otherworldly presence.

3. THE OMNISCIENCE OF GOD

In the closest connection with the omnipresence of God, faith finds itself confronted by the fact of the divine omniscience, which is given classic expression in Psalm 139. Because the omnipresence of God is the effective presence of the one who, in order to show his redeeming love, relates himself to the world, it cannot be conceived without the corresponding knowledge of the world and of everything that exists and occurs within it. For everything that exists and occurs in the world-system stands in a mutually determinative relation to humanity. Moreover, redemption, God's will to redeem, is not intended for humanity apart from the system in which humanity exists, the world over which it has been appointed, but precisely in this system. Therefore nothing in this system evades God's knowledge of the human person and of humanity as the object of his will to redeem. Everything to which God relates himself in his world-presence is, as an object of his will, also an object of his conscious awareness. Thus omniscience is connected at the same time with omnipotence, just as omnipotence and omnipresence are again connected with the attributes of God disclosed in revelation and determining his relation to the world. Faith in the wisdom, righteousness, and holiness of God is at the same time faith in his omniscience. It is God himself who in his wisdom determines and orders, for the purposes of his love, all the means and ways by which his active holiness and righteousness realize these purposes. Faith confidently affirms the scope of omniscience because it has experienced the power of revelation that demands and produces faith through the call of grace. Faith in the love that has sought and found the sinner, faith in the love that is active in free election, needs no long reflection in order to be faith in the one who knows the sinner and everything that concerns him, and so also his sins and cares, everything he does and leaves undone, his living and experiencing, the entire set of circumstances in which he stands. As faith in the one who has chosen him, it is faith in the one who did not first begin to know him only when he called him. God knew him in his entanglement in the kingdom of sin long before he showed himself to him in his electing love through the call of his word. That word, "the Lord knows those who are his" (2 Tim 2:19), thus extends beyond the circle of those who are his to those who are not his and to those who are not yet his. The hairs on all their heads are numbered, just like the stars (Isa 40:26–27) and the sparrows on the roof (Matt 10:29–30). Being convinced of the omniscience of God is not the result of reasoning but the certainty of faith in the God of redemption. It is an article of faith, as is belief in all of God's attributes, and as is faith itself, which is produced in us by God's revelation in Christ. From this it also becomes clear that revelation both assigns tasks to faith and supports faith in carrying them out. Revelation enables faith to stick to task when the burdensome reality of life in this world advises against doing so, as if there were people, with their doing and leaving undone, after whom God did not enquire and to whom he paid no attention (Ps 73:11).

It may appear that Christianity's belief in God's omniscience is an irrefutable certainty not primarily of faith, but of a guilty conscience. Belief in God's omnipresence may appear likewise and can be explained in the same way (66). Indeed, the guilty conscience's certainty of God's omniscience is so utterly compelling as to raise the problem of its compatibility with human freedom—a problem made more acute by reflection, as already appears in Stoic philosophy. Belief in divine omniscience was connected from the beginning with the endeavor to evade the force of this certainty. That this problem was already being addressed by philosophy before Christianity and beyond the sphere of revealed religion is testimony to the fact that God's omniscience was no stranger even to paganism. Belief in it was felt there far more distinctly than belief in God's world-presence, at least in a limited sense, which was no stranger either to paganism. These beliefs help to explain the pagan conscience, from which is derived that nameless fear that is the basis of all pagan religions. So while Ritschl is right to say that so-called natural religion never existed, he is wrong to insist that conscience was the result of moral or moral-religious development, the result of morality or religion. All missionary work confirms that Paul assesses the Gentiles more accurately when, despite the catalog of sins in Romans 1, he ascribes to them a conscience. One need only note what is implicit in the concept of conscience, that it is that self-awareness in which a person sees himself forced to come forward as a witness against himself. Self-awareness thus appears first and immediately as awareness of guilt, as awareness of liability to blame and judgment. Every Gentile who comes to faith testifies likewise, as does the anger of those who do not, that the gospel simply requires that we finally admit what we have already long known but refused to admit. This awareness is not aversion to "the new ideal for living." It is that same aversion that we find in the synagogue to testimony against oneself regarding one's own liability to blame and judgment. Only after the gospel had become his salvation did Paul dare to give expression to it in Romans 7 (34–35).

One can thus say that, of all the attributes of God, omniscience is the most generally known and acknowledged. But the Christian faith has something particular to say about it. Omniscience for Christianity is an active attribute that, like the other attributes, is effective in God's redeeming self-relation to the world. It is *the determination of his will and work for the world, or his action for and upon the world, as it is unveiled in revelation, through his knowledge of all that is and occurs*. Nevertheless, this does not imply that the creature first causes knowledge in God and so makes God to a certain extent dependent on it. Rather, *along with God's will for the creature, antecedent to the creature and to its conduct, God's knowledge concerning it is also posited and so precedes it*. God's knowledge is given along with the recognition that God's being is love, in which he desires to be what he is for a world that can only have its existence through him, so that his will for it is antecedent to it. For faith, this determination of God's knowledge of us is certain along with the fact of election as an eternal election, "before the foundation of the world" (Eph 1:4). God is not disposed to this election because of us, whether because of our existence or our conduct at any time. Rather, it first causes our existence and our conduct. Faith, as an object of God's knowledge, must therefore consider not merely the present or previous reality of life in this world and the world-system (Matt 10:30; 6:6; 1 John 3:20; Isa 29:15; 40:26; Ps 139:1–6; Heb 4:13). God's knowledge is foreknowledge (Matt 6:8; Acts 1:24; Ps 139:2,16), and therein lies its real significance for faith. It is inadequate to define omniscience as the perfection of God's knowledge of the world, for this does not portray omniscience as an active and effective attribute, and so neither does it express what is distinctive about it.

Foreknowledge is not *one* particular mode of divine knowledge of the world. It is *the* particular mode. For God's knowledge of the world is an active knowledge, and this activity is based on his will for us. Thus it holds here as well that the divine knowledge belongs to God's transcendence of the law of consistency that binds all creaturely knowledge, which is assembled from observation, inference, and estimation and finds consummate expression in science. It is not only in prophecy that God's knowledge is exercised as foreknowledge, but in all of his conduct in implementing his will for the world. Prophecy is but a particular expression of God's knowledge, and this not apart from God's will but as determined by it. As prophecy of future salvation, it is based exclusively on the will of God as this is ordered toward the future in connection with his knowledge. In connection with his will for the world, God knows its every detail, and he knows it in advance. He can thus, for example, put the prophet Jeremiah in the position to pronounce death upon the false prophets of Canaan, whose connection with God's will for the world consists in their response and relation to the work of the divinely commissioned prophet. The divine knowledge is foreknowledge, and it extends to everything that exists and occurs. Precisely because of this, it supports all who not only need to know that not even a drop in the bucket nor the dust on the scales is forgotten, but who must "enter into the sanctuary of God and perceive the end" (Ps 73:17), so that they may not lose heart. Neither sin nor any creature can ever bring to naught the counsel and will of God, for they can never escape his attention nor his power. This is the support of faith when the end is a long time coming. Herein also lies the connection between the omniscience and the wisdom of God. It is not as though omniscience were a result or effect of wisdom. Rather, it is only in wisdom that God watches all things that exist or occur, for he "knows the ways through waters deep."

Once the divine omniscience is seen as entirely foreknowledge, then the problem first really arises of its compatibility with human freedom. For now it is absolutely impossible to rest content with that saying, which is false anyway: "To major deeds the gods attend, the minor they ignore." Or, as others have put it, God only knows in advance the broad contours of history that he himself has determined in advance, while everything else is first known to him, so to speak, after the fact. Nor is the problem to be solved by appeal to God's transcendence of the temporal form of this-worldly being and occurrence. For by distinguishing God's knowledge as simultaneous from our knowledge as successive we have only exchanged one temporal form for another or for a spatial concept. Regardless, such a distinction cannot take away the fact that God's knowledge is indeed a knowledge of the succession of events to which we are bound, nor the fact that the divine knowledge looks down from above upon this-worldly occurrence. The divine knowledge seems to bear the sense of a compelling force not merely because of its temporal priority, but far more because of its categorical superiority. Because this-worldly occurrence, including all human action, lies beneath the divine knowledge, the inescapable assumption would appear to be that everything occurs inevitably and therefore necessarily.[4] The appeal to the distinction between necessity and certainty, such that the certainty that an event will occur does not imply its necessity, does not free us from the urgency of this problem either. This distinction only shows us what still remains to be demonstrated, without supplying the demonstration. The certainty of the divine foreknowledge is exactly what suggests the inalterability and thus necessity of what is foreknown and thus certain. This is especially the case with the certainty of the divine knowledge. For it does not rest, as does our certainty concerning something that has not yet happened, on its connection with premises that are clear to us, and so on a somehow discernible connection between cause and effect, premise and conclusion. It rests, rather, on God's immediate self-relation to that which exists and occurs. God knows in advance what will happen, and he knows it in its context but not through its context. He knows it through his superiority, his transcendence over it. This is why the divine foreknowledge appears to abolish our freedom. The question is whether we are compelled to affirm the proposition: If God knows it, it must happen.

What this proposition shows, however, is that if divine foreknowledge abolishes our freedom, it would do the same to God's freedom. What God knows, he would simply have to let happen. One could press the proposition further and claim that God also wills everything that he knows. But then God would also will sin, the very thing against which his entire self-manifestation is directed in his revelation. This would mean a still more complete demise of the freedom of his self-manifestation. If sin is necessary because God wills it, then so also is his revelation that is occasioned by sin. The same would hold for everything that exists and occurs, resulting in a system of determinism in which there is as little room for a living God as for human will and responsibility. Our freedom stands and falls with God's freedom. However disagreeable it may be to admit, we can assert the reality of our freedom only at the price of recognizing our sin. But it is only at the price of this recognition, and with it the recognition of our responsibility, that we can also assert our dignity. Our sin is not the will of God, and so it is

---

4. See the classic account of the history of the problem in Julius Müller, *Die christliche Lehre von der Sünde*, 6th ed. (Stuttgart, 1877) 3.2.2 (283–318); also Petavius, *Opus de theologicis dogmatibus*, 1.4.4–7.

not the work of God. Only our faith is the will of God, and so also the work of God. And thus is our sin the greater if we refuse him.

But now we stand before a new problem. We experience our own sin, our act, which we must recognize and acknowledge to be the opposite of God's will, at the same time as the result of a compulsion that weighs upon us. We cannot escape sin—and how can we explain this? Does this not indeed abolish once again the conclusion we had just reached, that our freedom is not compromised by the divine omniscience? On the one hand, we experience that God offers himself to us for redemption, that he himself produces the faith he demands, and that we remain under the power of sin if we refuse faith. This convinces us that God does not will sin, so that sin cannot be the result of a compulsion proceeding from him. On the other hand, we experience that, "when I want to do good, I find that evil lies close at hand" (Rom 7:21). The systems of nature and history force it upon us. This appears to be the price at which we may live within history. If we have had to tell ourselves that everything that exists and occurs can only do so if God acts effectively upon the world-system, does this not indeed imply that the necessity of sin has been ordained by him? This is indeed what Luther emphasized in *The Bondage of the Will*. Was Luther wrong? The answer we have to give can only be that it is by no means sin, but the compulsion that we experience, that is willed and ordained by God. God does not will sin. This is certain from the demand for faith that we experience from his revelation in his action toward us. It is not the fact of sin's existence in the world that rests on God's will, but the manner in which it does so. Sin would have no dominion in the world, and God would show no patience toward it, if he did not desire to redeem us. That sin is so utterly in the world as we experience it to be, as a power that forces us under its control—this belongs to the ways ordered by God's wisdom. We are meant to suffer it so that we grow sick of it. One thinks of Paul's comment about the law of God, that it "entered in, so that sin might grow more powerful" and "all the world be guilty before God" (Rom 5:20; 3:19). God knows about sin before it exists or occurs. He does not counteract it, so that it may happen. He even sustains the world-system in nature and history, the very system in which sin forces us under its control, because he desires not to abandon the world, but to redeem it. Through his revelation he now sets before us the decision whether we will remain in sin, adding sin to sin, and in this way lets us experience that his will and his work are and must be our freedom, while our sin is our own work entirely.

From all this we also conclude that if God's foreknowledge appears to annihilate our freedom, it is merely appearance, not reality. Only one annihilation of freedom proceeds from God: when God's judgment turns against those who "were not willing" as they could and should have been (Matt 23:37; Luke 13:34). The question concerning the relationship between our freedom and the divine foreknowledge thus becomes more urgent as touching the one free act upon which all else depends, the question concerning the faith that God requires and gives. Nothing that we do before coming to faith is free to the extent that faith is. When faith is offered to us, then we really stand before the decisive act. Then also is there really possible for us that act which is solely and entirely ours: not faith, but unbelief. Unbelief alone is our act. That is why it constitutes the decisive sin, the sin in which all other sins "are retained" against us (John 20:23). If even faith, though brought about by God, is not forced upon us by God, how much less unbelief. If we are certain of this, we also know that the appearance of the annihilation of our freedom by the divine foreknowledge is only an appearance. It belongs to the temptation with which faith must struggle and which can only be overcome by faith. This temptation emerges from the force exerted by sin and by sin's dominion over us in the world and in history. But for those who have really overcome it, this temptation, which lies merely in the realm of thought, is easy to overcome.

That which compromises or abolishes our freedom, that which now causes us to suffer under the lack of freedom, is something entirely other than the omniscience of God. Because omniscience does not do this, it follows that omniscience extends not merely to that which becomes reality through our conduct, but also to the result of conduct other than what we have chosen. Not only do Old Testament passages express this (1 Sam 23:10–13; Jer 38:17–20; Ezek 3:6). Jesus himself also testifies to it. What he says about the hypothetical repentance of Tyre and Sidon, Sodom and Gomorrah (Matt 11:20–24) is just as true for him as his judgment over the actual sin of Capernaum, Chorazin, and Bethsaida. The occasion and purpose of his words show that they cannot be taken as mere rhetorical flourish rather than truth. For if it is not the truth that Jesus speaks about those cities on which God's judgments once fell, then the cities he now chastises need not heed his verdict.

4. THE ETERNITY AND IMMUTABILITY OF GOD

Holiness, righteousness, wisdom, omnipotence, omnipresence, omniscience—these are the attributes of the one who in his revelation wonderfully manifests himself for our redemption, the Father of our Lord Jesus Christ, who alone is God. As we recognize him as God in these attributes, he binds us to faith, he brings about faith in us and sustains it, and he offers us redemption as the solution to the actual riddle of the world. This is the riddle of history, which everyone carries around in his own person and history, even if for a long time, like Percival, he does not know to ask the question to which he must find an answer. Through the exercise of these attributes in and through the one whom he sent to carry out his counsel, through Jesus the Christ, he saves our life from destruction. In this way we see for the first time that we do not possess our life for no purpose, and that a world that in itself can only perish still does not exist for no purpose. We exist in order to experience that God is love. We are here so that God may be, for us and in his fellowship with us, everything that he is, "so that our fellowship may be fellowship with the Father and with his Son Jesus Christ" through the Holy Spirit (1 John 1:3). In this fellowship our life is saved from destruction, for God has bound it to himself and united himself with us. Our life thus becomes like that of the Mediator, like the life of God himself an "indestructible life" (Heb 7:16), saved not merely from the law of sin and death, but exalted with our God over the law of becoming and passing away. It has become eternal life. Contingency remains. Life is and remains dependent, conditioned by God, by his love. But the contingency of life is only a matter of its having come into existence and its continuation. Passing away is excluded by God's loving fellowship with us, in which we are "the purpose of God." Thus, as God brings about our eternal life, his own eternity presents itself to our experience as a final divine attribute. In this way we recognize for the first time what God's eternity is.

Everywhere that God is sought, even in paganism, there is found the idea of the eternity of the deity. It is inseparable from the idea of God, from the idea of the power that is superior to the world (Rom 1:20,23). That is why among the Greeks, for example, immortality is the predicate of the gods in contrast to human "mortals." But such immortality is by no means absolute transcendence over death.[5] In the Germanic myths, even the

---

5. Karl-Friedrich von Nägelsbach, *Homerische Theologie*, 3rd ed., rev. Georg Autenrieth (Nuremberg, 1884) §§11–12 (pp. 32–34); Nägelsbach, *Nachhomerische Theologie* (Nuremberg, 1857) §§6–8 (pp. 9–15).

deities fall victim to the destruction of the world. If the notion of what lies "beyond the twilight of the gods" is ever expressed, it is not the gods. For twilight is brought about by the rising of a new world and the gods' own rising again. Man seeks deity in order to save himself by it. This is basically the entire notion of eternity that one finds in paganism, and one can probably find no other, unless one resorts to the Nirvana of Indian religion. For the idea of an endless duration—the only concept with which one can reckon—is still ultimately unbearable.

The eternity that God opens up to us in his revelation is a different matter. First of all, it too is an active, effective attribute of God. It is that transcendence of God over the law of creaturely being, which manifests itself by lifting our life above the law of becoming and passing away. Or it is the exercise of his transcendence over the law of becoming and passing away upon us and upon our life. In doing so, he makes us partakers of his life and joins himself with us and us with himself. The law of becoming and passing away, our being limited to the temporal form of creaturely being, does not prevent him from being for us everything that he is, from joining himself with us and thereby filling our life with content that is not subject to this law. It thus becomes clear for the first time what the purpose of our existence is, and particularly what the purpose of a created world is. God's creation is not destined to pass away, but to remain. For it is destined to be the object of God's love as he relates himself to us. The reality of the world-system that weighs down upon us would certainly not have us grasp this destiny. The revelation of God, however, lets us recognize that the goal of the ways of his love is neither the development of the world, nor its destruction, but rather its transformation—a transformation in which, admittedly, what has become of the world in the system of history, and what has been made of the world by us, must and will perish.

The eternity of God is thus a terror to our conscience as long as we have not yet understood the full content and purpose of his revelation. This is just as understandable as the comparable effect of the other attributes of God. But it becomes a truly culpable misconception, the "sin of the consciousness of guilt," if one persists in it and refuses him who, in judgment and in grace, desires to bring us to awareness of both his eternity and all his attributes, his will and his power, so that we might believe in him.

Now if what has been said above captures the significance of the eternity of God, if the recognition of eternity is the crowning achievement of our knowledge of the attributes of God, then we understand why eternity undeniably appears almost as often in the praise and worship of the congregation as does the power of God (Rom 11:36; 16:26–27; 2 Cor 11:31; Eph 3:21; Phil 4:20; 1 Tim 1:17; 6:16; 2 Tim 4:18; Heb 9:14; 13:21; 1 Pet 4:11; 5:11; Rev 1:4,8; Isa 41:4; 43:10; 48:12; Ps 90:2). For faith, the certainty of eternity is a certainty of security in God. The ultimate experience of the strong and saving righteousness of God thus places on the lips of the congregation the praise of God's power and eternity. This is all the more the case because all of God's action for us and upon us is the expression and execution of his will which is settled in his being, not merely emerging in history but transcending it, and existing before the world. It is the expression of God's self-determination before the world and its time, to be for the world, and thereby the determination of the world or rather its community for him. It is impossible for faith to think of God's will for us as other than eternal. This is why expressions such as Rom 16:25–27; Eph 3:19–21; 2 Tim 1:9; Tit 1:2; Eph 1:4; Matt 13:35; 25:34; and 1 Pet 1:20 are legitimate and cannot be regarded as mere opinions of the New Testament authors. This eternity of God guarantees the future and is the refuge of the one who prays (Ps 90:2; Rom 11:36). Eternity, like all God's attributes, is an article of faith, but it is just as certain for faith as faith itself. For faith arises only through truth, through the reality of its object, and it *has* the truth.

The difficulty of imagining eternity does not make faith any less sure of it. On the contrary, faith clearly considers the fact that eternity is something entirely other than the form of existence to which we in this present world-system are bound—until it appears what we shall be (1 John 3:2). Yet we must still try to make clear to ourselves what eternity is. With God, we must rule out beginning and ending, having come in to being, becoming, and passing away. Because of this, and as already implied in his transcendence over the law of our existence, God also transcends the nature of time and the succession of moments. Time exists not in him, but only in his presence. That is why he is the Lord of time, and why a thousand years are like a day to him, and a day like a thousand years. Eternity therefore cannot be imagined as an eternity of succession or as sempiternity, and so as an infinite sequence of moments—an absurdity, for an infinite succession of finites is a contradiction in terms. Eternity may at best be imagined, with Augustine, as an eternity of simultaneity, though this concept too is only an exchange of one representation of time for another, or of a temporal representation with a spatial. Another way presents itself to us, however, both to attain to the actual concept of eternity as well as to recognize that there is something even in our own life by which we may perceive something of what eternity is.

Because God's eternity excludes his having come in to being and his becoming and thus past and future, it shows itself as the reality of the concept of the present. For us, the present is only the mathematical point at which the future flows into the past, its arrival vanishing at once and becoming instantly unavailable. Thus, in the course of our existence, there is no present that can be held on to. Only at one point, not of our existence but of our personal being, is there a present at which we can become acquainted with what the present is. This point is in our conscience, indeed, in our guilty conscience. In it we are conscious of ourselves in such a way that we must say of our sin not "I *was* the one," but "I *am* the one who has done this." The past of the deed and the continuing sameness of the person so bind themselves together that the deed does not in fact pass away. In our conscience we remain not merely notionally but actually present to ourselves. In conscience, even our future is already our present. In conscience, the past is not past nor the future, future. This is how we know what that present is that will never become the past and in which we already live and experience the future. Through the forgiveness of sins, and thus in trusting possession of the redeeming love of God, the past fades away. But for all that does flow inexorably from the present into the past, one thing does not: the saved life, in which the future for which we wait is at the same time already the present. As we know in our guilty conscience what eternal death is, since it is in us, so we know in our conscience as it has been set free by forgiveness what eternal life is, since it too is in us. In this way we form an image, even if only a distant one, of the eternity of God. It is that being which corresponds perfectly to personal life, a being towards which we too have been created and redeemed, an everlasting, blessed being in the full vigor of life, in eternal youth, 2 Cor 4:16–18.

Eternity therefore belongs among those attributes of God in which he enacts his being for us. It is thus no mere formal concept for indicating his mode of being in distinction from the temporal form of creaturely being. Rather, it includes the material affirmation of God's immutability, along with the impossibility of his ever having been other than he is. For everything about him that we have recognized so far, he so enacts in his eternity that it will endure despite the opposition of our sin to his will. In wonderful transcendence over the law of consistency, and yet without negating this law, he maintains what he is and wills to be, and thus proves, against the opposition that he encounters in us, that nothing can change him or his will (Rom 16:26; Mal 3:6; Num 23:19; Ps 102:26–27). The triumph of sin or of the sinful creature over him is utterly excluded. Sin does evoke his opposition, and his action for us thus takes on a particular character, in that his will to create becomes a will to redeem. But this does not bring about a change of either his being or even his attitude towards the world. It results only in his remaining like himself in his love and his remaining the same for us precisely in this love. This does not exclude a diversity in the working of his love. Rather, it confirms the constancy of this same love in the wealth of its manifestations. We saw earlier that human freedom does not constitute any limitation on God, but actually serves to display God's power and freedom still more gloriously. This already implies the immutability of God, which of course had to conduct itself toward the misuse of freedom differently than if it had been bound to the law of consistency. But as the immutability of his love it is able to act differently without itself becoming different. Even his revelation in Christ—indeed, precisely this—has no other purpose and achieves no other success than the demonstration and confirmation that God desires to be for us and in association with us everything that he is. God's eternal relation to us became a particular appearance to accomplish the task love had set for itself: to counteract sin and death. Of this appearance, the content is the same, the subject is the same, and the attributes are the same. Only the manner of its appearing differs, as it takes particular form for its task, so that it would have been otherwise had there been no sin. It is the task of Christology to show how the immutability of God, and with it all of his attributes, appear in Christ—indeed, appear just as wonderfully as in God's continuing to love us despite our sin. The one is just as wonderful as the other, and each is only to be known from the reality in which it appears. The understanding of immutability that one might derive merely from the concept of God is something entirely different than what God enacts in his revelation and through which he binds us to faith and bolsters us in it.

That God shows himself in his revelation as eternal and immutable is of particular significance for the question of the truth of the knowledge of God brought about through revelation. For now it follows that God, whose revelation is at the same time his self-assertion against sin, is nothing other, and is not other, than how he manifests himself to be. The attributes that we discern in his revelation are the attributes of his being. To be sure, they are the attributes of his being in his relation to us, but this is a relation in which he wills to be for us everything that he is. Precisely because he wills to be for us everything that he is, it is not merely something about him that we can and should perceive. Above and beyond this relation to us he can be no different than he is in it. What still lies beyond our present knowledge is related to what we repeatedly imagine about the significance of mission and the activity of God's world-presence. The difference between our present and future knowledge rests on the fact that the time of the offer of salvation still continues and the consummation of salvation only begins with the final judgment of the saving righteousness of God. We can only repeat here what was said in our preliminary investigations: how it comes about that God exists exceeds our intellectual capacity, as do other things that are perceived in the sphere of knowledge of this world. But what he is and how he is, his reality—this he gives us to know, and that action through which we know him is faith, to which he binds us and which he brings about in us. What we know in faith, however, is the truth, and it will not do continually to stress only the boundaries and limitations instead of the truth and riches of our knowledge. Of course, as one progresses from faith to faith, so also from knowledge to knowledge, and for this reason there is a difference between our earthly and heavenly knowledge, according to Paul's statement in 1 Corinthians 13:12. We will then receive many shameful corrections. But what we have truly known in and through faith will be fully and exuberantly confirmed.

5

The Unity of the Divine Attributes, or the Glory of God

In every attribute the entire, undivided being of God is active. In each, all of the other attributes are co-posited and co-effective. The attributes do not indicate different actions of God detached from or operating alongside each other. Otherwise one would speak of the necessity of balancing certain attributes with each other, such as grace and mercy with righteousness, or of a temporary suspension of righteousness through the patience of God, or of a self-limitation of God in the renunciation of the unlimited exercise of his power, or of a temporary restraint of his opposition to sin. But not only can there be no such talk of restraint or self-limitation, but still less is there any need for a balancing of different attributes. As patience is an activity of God's wisdom, so grace is an exercise of his righteousness. The will of God exercised in all of his attributes is one that counteracts sin for the purpose of his love, and the defining characteristic of all the attributes is the self-manifestation of God in the unity of judgment and grace for the purpose of redemption. This is the unity of his attributes, in which appears his relation to us or his being in his conduct toward us. For this unity religion has designated the concept of the glory of God, כָּבוֹד or δόξα. According to Exodus 33:18–19 it is "all the goodness of YHWH." It is glory that should and does rise over Israel in the fulfillment of the promise (Isa 40:5; 46:13; 60:1) and that gives itself to be known in Christ (2 Cor 4:6; Heb 1:3), not only in what God does to Christ (Rom 6:4), but in what Christ is for us.

The attributes of God are not a law of his being operating on its own, on the analogy of a power of nature, with inner necessity or in simple consistency. They are the appearance of his will as it acts in freedom, of his transcendence over the law of consistency. His conduct is consistent, but it does not proceed according to a law of consistency. In this transcendence over the law of consistency he is active against the law of sin and death at work in our history, for the purpose of realizing his loving fellowship with us. It is his wisdom that finds the ways to this end, first of all in sustaining and carrying the world in the omnipotence of his love, so that it might suffer under the law of sin and death and so be made ready to receive his self-offering in faith and to experience redemption. And the ways he chooses in order to offer himself to us are the ways of electing love. Upon these ways there appears the full grandeur, power, and freedom of his love, so that here and here alone the full power of sin can and does make itself felt in its struggle against him. So it comes to pass that God's self-manifestation for our redemption has a history. It begins with his preservation of the sinful world, finds its mid-point in God's revelation in Christ, and reaches its conclusion in the judgment of his mighty, saving righteousness upon the community of the elect. It is a unified action of God, not by means of history, but within history. In this history, humanity will and must perish in itself, insofar as it does not accept God's action in faith for redemption.

This unified action of God for the purpose of our redemption is to this day and will be to the end a historical and efficacious action. In it the evangelization of the world is joined to the revelation of Christ. This explains why, on the one hand, all of God's attributes are always at work in this action, and why, on the other, these attributes are only perceived and recognized within the sphere of revelation, and nevertheless in such a way that even there their appearing becomes ever more complete, the more completely God is active. This is related to what we had to say regarding God's one, identical world-presence and its particular manifestations, and regarding the difference between omnipresence and saving presence, etc. This is why the revelation of the glory of God is the object of the promise and hope of Israel, and why glory attends the proclamation of the birth of Christ (Luke 2:9), becomes present in Christ (John 1:14; 2:11), is displayed in his resurrection through his vindication (Rom 6:4; 1 Tim 3:16), and yet appears in full force only at his second coming (Matt 16:27; 19:28; 25:31; 2 Thess 1:9–10). Glory attests itself in the gospel (1 Tim 1:11), is active especially on and in the community through the presence of the Holy Spirit

(Eph 3:16; Col 1:11; 1 Tim 4:14), and forms the final goal of Christian hope. The distinction and the unity of our present and future knowledge of God are connected with this historical appearing of the glory of God, as noted above (81), and to both there applies what God demands and produces in his revelation: "if you believe, you will see the glory of God" (John 11:40).

Name Index

Subject Index

CPSIA information can be obtained
at www.ICGtesting.com
Printed in the USA
BVOW06*0228030717

488302BV00005B/16/P